S0-ADS-711

IF YOU DON'T LIKE THE NEWS...

Go Out and Make Some of Your Own

IF YOU DON'T LIKE THE NEWS...

GO OUT AND

MAKE SOME

OF YOUR OWN

Wes "Scoop" Nisker

TEN SPEED PRESS BERKELEY, CALIFORNIA

TEN SPEED PRESS
P.O. Box 7123
Berkeley, California 94707

Cover design by Fifth Street Design
Text design by Sarah Levin

Library of Congress Cataloging-in-Publication Data

Nisker, Wes.
    If you don't like the news—go out and make some of your own / Wes "Scoop" Nisker.
        p.   cm.
    ISBN 0-89815-626-2 : $14.95
    1. Nisker, Wes. 2. Radio journalists—United States—Biography.
    I. Title.
    PN4874.N57A3   1994
    070'.92—dc20   94-26664
    (B)   CIP

Printed in the United States of America
1 2 3 4 5—98 97 96 95 94

This book is dedicated to my daughter,
Rose, and to all of her generation.
Question authority. Question reality.
And may all manner of things
be well with you.

ACKNOWLEDGMENTS

My deepest gratitude to the two people who guided me through my first book, *Crazy Wisdom*, and now this book as well: to Shoshana Alexander for her extraordinary editorial skills, which include vision, spunk, and a cosmic sense of humor; and to Mariah Bear for her vast knowledge of everything, her great wit, and her patience in helping me find my voice on paper. I also want to express my appreciation to Sarah Levin for designing both *Crazy Wisdom* and this book, making them so beautiful and user-friendly. And to Phil Wood, George Young, and all the folks at Ten Speed Press—after listening to other authors, I have a feeling that I got lucky this lifetime, and landed in publishing heaven. Thank you all so much.

Also special love and thanks to Barbara Gates, Alan Novidor, and Dewey Livingston, my collaborators on the Buddhist journal *Inquiring Mind*, and to all the "Mind" readers who may have seen early versions of some parts of this book in my columns; to my friend Paul Krassner, who embodies crazy wisdom and brings it to life in our Esalen workshops; and to Darryl Henriques, for his collaboration and friendship over the years, and especially for incarnating as the Swami from Miami. I would also like to acknowledge my colleagues and friends at "Jive 95," the old KSAN–FM, in San Francisco, and at KFOG–FM, along with all the "jivers" and "fogheads" who have lent me their ears and their encouragement over the past decade. My deepest love and gratitude to my sweet sister Jan and her kids, and to Mudita, Dan, Jeff, Perry, Steven, Laurinda and all my Harwood housemates, Nina, Suzie, Catherine, Lynn, Ron, Ed, Sylvia, Tessa and Brian, Robert and Djuna, Lloyd and Abby, Jerry and Elizabeth, and to all the people who have lived through parts of this book with me. Also, deep bows of respect and love to my dear friends and benefactors, Jack Kornfield and Joseph Goldstein. And finally, heartfelt love and thanks to my partner, Terry. During the writing of this book she kept bringing me back to the present moment, and so often made those moments sweet.

CONTENTS

I knew then, and I know now, it is no use trying to do anything—I speak only for myself—publicly. It is no use trying merely to modify present forms. The whole great form of our era will have to go. And nothing will really send it down but the new shoots of life springing up and slowly bursting the foundations. And one can do nothing but fight tooth and nail to defend the new shoots of life from being crushed out, and let them grow. We can't make life. We can but fight for the life that grows in us.

D. H. LAWRENCE, NOTE TO *"THE CROWN"*

Love tells me I'm everything.
Wisdom tells me I'm nothing.
And between the two my life flows.

SRI NISARGADATTA

WHERE I AM COMING FROM

Chapter One

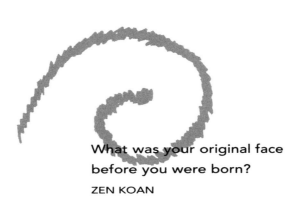

What was your original face
before you were born?
ZEN KOAN

When I think back on my origins, I am reminded of the notion, popular in twentieth-century physics, that there are no beginnings—or middles or endings either. In this view of our space-time continuum, everything happens simultaneously, so it's always everybody's birthday. And happy birthday to you too.

Conventionally speaking, I was born in a small Nebraska town on December 22nd, 1942, just ahead of the baby boom. My Jewish immigrant parents were happy to have a son, and no doubt had high hopes for me. They could never have imagined that I would one day reject their god and their religion, incite riots against the government of their adopted country, and even come to question the overall worth of our species. What a son I turned out to be! But then, what a space-time I was born into—America in the last half of the twentieth century.

Like many members of my generation, I have long been obsessed with studying myself, and have spent a good deal of time and money tracing the roots of my lifelong sense of alienation. Just being alive in this time of rapid change is enough to make anyone feel a little disconnected, but we each have our personal stories to explain the phenomena. I have come to believe that growing up as the only Jewish kid in a small midwestern town got me started feeling like an outsider, a stance which eventually led me into league with the world's radicals and mockers, and then into Buddhism, where detachment itself is considered a state of grace. All this, perhaps, because of being the only kid in my home town who didn't believe in Jesus.

For a while, when I was a young boy, there were just enough Jews in Norfolk, Nebraska, to keep a little synagogue going above the town bakery. As I remember, you walked around behind the bread ovens and up a flight of wooden stairs to a large room with wood-slat walls. At one end of the room stood the Torah and facing it, a few benches. I can recall the bakery smells wafting up to this makeshift synagogue on Friday nights and making it very difficult to fast on Yom Kippur. But then two of Norfolk's Jewish families moved away in the early 1950s, leaving too few Jewish males in town for a minyan, the minimum number who must be praying before God will listen. After the synagogue over the bakery closed down, my Jewish education had to come to me by stagecoach.

To prepare me for my bar mitzvah, my parents hired a "circuit rabbi." He traveled through the small towns of Iowa and Nebraska by Greyhound bus, teaching and ministering to the lost Jewish tribes of the American Midwest. His name was Rabbi Falik, and while that moniker alone could have kept him from getting his own pulpit and congregation, his physical appearance didn't help any. His face was dominated by an enormous nose, which vied for one's attention with bulging, red-rimmed eyes. He had a constant dampness around his mouth and smelled strongly of musty old-world synagogues and garlic—always of garlic.

Once a week, the Greyhound would let Rabbi Falik off right in front of my house for my bar mitzvah lesson. I didn't want other kids to see this strange, medieval-looking man coming to visit, so whenever he was due I would lure them away from our neighborhood, then make up some excuse to run back home just in time to meet the bus and rush the rabbi inside.

My bar mitzvah lessons involved memorizing long passages of Hebraic script that made no sense to me, in preparation to join a Jewish community that, in my home town at least, did not exist. My entire rite of passage and spiritual initiation were thus almost completely devoid of meaning.

In order to take part in the rituals that *did* matter to young people in Norfolk, I had to become a mock Christian. For instance, as a member of the junior-high-school choir, I joined in singing hymns and carols at the annual Christmas vespers program. However, when the songs mentioned Jesus as "our lord" or "savior," I always crossed my fingers. I wanted Jehovah to know that I had not fallen for this Jesus hoax, that I was still waiting for the *real* messiah to come. I'm still waiting.

My mother felt guilty that we didn't live among other Jews, and she struggled to pull off Jewish rituals in our house, especially around Christmas time. Although we had an evergreen like everybody else, decorated with Christmas-tree lights, my mother always put a Star of David on top and called it a "Chanukkah bush." I remember taking some pride in the fact that we Jews had one more point on our star than the Christians.

My parents had ended up in Norfolk during the Depression. One of my mother's relatives—a stereotypical wandering Jewish rag salesman—wandered all the way over from Russia to this little Nebraska town, where he opened a clothing store. He asked my father if he wanted to open up a shoe department in the store. Times were hard and my father needed work, so, even though he knew nothing about shoes, he accepted the offer and suddenly found himself fitting flats, wedgies, and high heels onto the feet of German and Polish farm wives. My parents planned to wait out the Depression in Norfolk and then move back to Minneapolis where, as my mother would wistfully say, "there are more Yiddishkeit." But one thing led to another, and before you knew it my father had his very own store, Nisker's Shoes and Accessories, right there on Main

Street, and had joined the Norfolk Country Club, the Lions Club, and even the Masonic Lodge. It is somehow appropriate that a bloodline of Jews who were driven out of their Middle Eastern homeland two millenia ago would eventually arrive in the American Midwest, only to get involved with the Masons, a Middle Eastern mystery cult.

In some ways, my father's childhood was not that different from my own. He grew up in a village outside of Warsaw, Poland, where he too was one of the few Jewish kids in a rural Christian community. His parents owned a small grocery store and, according to my father, lived very simply, just a half-step up from the peasantry. This should come as no surprise. After all, as recently as 1906, the year my father was born, the majority of the world's people were still simple peasants. For most of history, only kings and queens have lived in the style to which so many of us today have grown accustomed.

My father understood this well. After he had become a successful middle-class merchant in America, he would say to his children, "We live like kings here." We never did believe him, mostly because we had even greater expectations for our lives. We grew up thinking we could become anyone we wanted to be; we could have it all.

A certain sort of homelessness must be embedded in the Jewish genes by now. My early ancestors were kicked out of their land of milk and honey, and subsequent generations of Jews could hardly feel at home in their European home towns. They lived with the constant threat of being uprooted by wars and pogroms. In contrast, I chose to leave home in search of one utopian dream or another. I turned *myself* into a refugee. Homelessness of various kinds is endemic in this highly mobile century. We have indeed become a global village, but along the way we lost our villages.

All the while I was growing up, I knew that I would someday move away from Norfolk, Nebraska. This small farming community was no place for an educated, ambitious Jewish boy. Furthermore, there were no Jewish girls in town, and I wouldn't be allowed to marry and settle down with one of the local shiksas. Although ideally my parents would have wanted me to take over their shoe store, they always knew—and even hoped—that I would someday make my life in a city with a Jewish community, a *big* city like Omaha or Minneapolis. I grew up knowing that my home town would never become my "home."

Perhaps because of this, my entire life became a search for home, or maybe for a sort of divine homelessness, an inner acceptance of the fact that there is never any solid ground to stand on, and no place to call one's own.

> *If you were born in the last fifty years, you have ten times as much chance of being seriously depressed as you would if you were born in the fifty years before that time.*
>
> NATIONAL INSTITUTE OF MENTAL HEALTH, 1988

My generation is full of stories about feeling rootless and confused in the midst of twentieth-century upheavals. Although most of us were given all the physical comforts we needed, we often suffered tremendous metaphysical discomfort. As the saying goes, if it isn't one thing, it's another.

The final half of this century has been a high-speed ride through the Atomic Age, the Television Age, the Information Age, the Space Age, the Computer Age, and, last but not least, the Age of Anxiety. Things have changed so rapidly that our lives often seem to be dominated by nostalgia. Even if we didn't leave home, home left us.

It was only back in the 1500s that humans even started measuring time in hundred-year periods called centuries. These days, it moves so fast that we measure history in decades, stamping each one with its own character. It does appear, however, that things may have begun slowing down lately—at least it seems to have been the "me decade" for quite a while now.

My generation arrived in a time of deconstruction and disruption. By now, everybody seems rootless and everything lies broken in pieces: mountains, forests, nations, families, dreams, beliefs, atoms—all shattered and scattered. When I was young, chaos was something bad that might be avoided if you were careful, not a theory to explain the laws of nature.

This should be called the Century of Deconstruction. Within the past one hundred years, Freud and his legions took apart the human psyche; Einstein and his colleagues broke matter into many strange, invisible particles; Wittgenstein and others, including such artists as Beckett and Burroughs, took language apart until it dissolved back into itself, without meaning or point of reference; biologists separated the body into tiny coded molecules that seem to prove we are at the mercy of evolution; anthropologists and historians took apart the past, showing progress to be little more than a ruling-class rationale for bloodletting; technology in all its various forms—bombs, automobiles, airplanes, radios, and televisions—blew us, flew us, and drew us away from our homes toward a global village that has no center and no traditions. Meanwhile, burgeoning humanity, hungry for more living space, food, security, and amusement, is tearing apart mother earth, leaving her disfigured and broken in pieces. It's been a century of deconstruction, all right, and all the king's horses and all the king's men may not be able to put Humpty together again.

Many members of the baby-boom generation who grew up in this shattering world have since been wandering through the wreckage, trying to assemble some metaphysical sanity. Some of what we've found to believe in may seem superstitious or silly, but we desperately needed something to hold onto besides our material possessions. We began searching for a new philosophy of wholeness, and for reconnection with our own bodies, with each other, with nature, and with the cosmos. The search led many of us far from our Judeo-Christian roots and superpower citizenship, into foreign religions, anarchist politics, past lives, even to the stars.

Over the years, I and many of my friends have had an interest in astrology, something totally alien to my family. One day, after I had acquired long hair and a strange look in my eyes, I informed my mother that I was a Capricorn. She frowned at me and said, "No you're not. You're still Jewish."

Although I don't give astrology a whole lot of credence, I do know that my fellow Capricorns include Richard Nixon and Chairman Mao, and an astrologer did tell me once that this sign tends toward megalomania. Maybe that's why I always believed that whatever I am doing, I'm taking part in some kind of world-shaking revolution. My stars may also have something to do with my obsession with trying to make sense of this life. Then again, such beliefs may just come from having lived through such confusing, transitional times.

There is another, more humbling aspect of my astrological sign. Capricorn is represented by the goat, traditionally a sacrificial animal. The Jewish patriarch Abraham killed a goat in place of his son, and at the Kali Temple in Calcutta, India, I saw a goat's heart being cut out to please the dark goddess. Both gods and goddesses seem to like offerings of goat. On the other hand, you could say that in the end everyone and everything is sacrificed to one deity or another.

When I was growing up, I thought it would have been exciting to be born three days later and have the same birthday as Jesus. Since becoming more of a neo-pagan, however, I have grown quite proud of being born on December 22nd, which is also the birthday of the sun. Not the Son of God, but the firey sun who art in heaven, hallowed be thy light. The sun that is the star of our whole show. Every year on my birthday, the day after the winter solstice, the sun starts to rise earlier and earlier and stick around later and later, in answer to the pagans' prayers. My birthday—the sun's birthday—is the rebirth of light and hope. It should be a day of rejoicing like no other.

I've run into some other fascinating theories to explain why I am who

I am. A Tibetan holy man once told me that I was probably the reincarnation of an Eastern European Jew who had been killed in a Nazi concentration camp. According to this Tibetan, I suffered so much under the Nazis that a lot of my negative karma was burned away. That's why I was rewarded with rebirth here in America, the land of the free and the home of the plenty. In this life, I have indeed been given great physical comforts, copious education, and enough money and leisure time to discover the teachings of the Buddha, setting me on the path to complete liberation from the rounds of rebirth. In other words, if I use this new incarnation well and become fully enlightened, I won't have to be born again in Germany, America, or even Tibet. I will be freed from what beat Buddhist Jack Kerouac called "the wheel of the quivering meat conception."

I'm not sure whether or not I believe in such stories about rebirth. Reincarnation might just be another of the fictions humans invent to make sense of this puzzling existence and the apparent lack of justice in the world. Then again, if there *is* rebirth, maybe I should keep my nose relatively clean during this lifetime to ensure that my next one is quite spectacular.

New species have come on the stage slowly and at successive intervals; and the amount of change, after equal intervals of time, is widely different in different groups. The extinction of species and of whole groups of species, which has played so conspicuous a part in the history of the organic world, almost inevitably follows on the principle of natural selection; for old forms will be supplanted by new and improved forms.

CHARLES DARWIN, *ON THE ORIGIN OF SPECIES*

Living in the last half of the twentieth century, we have been exposed to some very, very large perspectives on life. To me, these pictures of vastness are the major solace modern science can offer us, perhaps in exchange for having taken so much away. The fact that I am able to see myself as part of a movement or epoch, or as a participant in a stage of biological or cosmic evolution, gives some relief from the personal.

In my life to date, I have seen live footage of the earth from the moon, and have learned about the existence of millions of galaxies other than my own, full of billions of stars. Only recently have we even become familiar with such *numbers*. When I was growing up, kids used "billions" to mean "humungous." Now we talk about the national debt in trillions, and we know there are trillions of stars, at the very least. Maybe there are really quadrillions of stars, and soon we'll discover there are even pentillions, and before you know it, we'll be talking serious stars.

Another big perspective, that of modern biology and anthropology, allows us to trace the human family tree back to australopithecus, an early ape-man who appeared on the scene in southern Africa about five million years ago. Australopithecus was the first to come down from the trees and head for the local tavern, after stopping off briefly in the plains to grow some grain and hops. Specimens of australiopithecus can still be found drinking beer in all corners of the planet.

I can imagine myself as a more recent ancestor, Homo habilis, the "handyman." He came along about three million years ago, and started standing upright more often, probably in order to throw a rock at some moving protein or fix a leaky roof. Biologists say that straightening up like this could have caused the enormous increase in brain size between australopithecus and Homo habilis. In other words, we began standing upright and got smart at the same time. Now maybe our brains are big enough and it's time for us to lie down for a while.

Still, it must have been very exciting to stand up, because the next thing you know, our ancestors were standing up all the time. We became Homo erectus, or "upright humans," and we're not talking about morality here. In fact, because Homo erectus kept on standing, even in polite company, their genitalia and breasts were suddenly right out there in front for everyone to see. The fig leaf, loincloth, and brassiere must have been invented soon after.

Our closest relatives, Homo sapiens neanderthalensis (the Neanderthals), appeared about 300,000 years ago. They are the first to be called Homo sapiens, in great part because they had burial rituals. In other words, they were the first of our kind to become aware of their own death. They were "self" conscious. It seems strange to me that, on one hand, we are very proud of having developed this self-consciousness, and yet it is also the evolutionary moment we refer to as "the fall." Maybe we should decide whether we like self-consciousness or not, although I doubt there is much we can do about it. Many of my generation have tried to dissolve their sense of being a separate self, and have found it the most difficult of all endeavors.

Some scientists have come to believe that we are now a completely new species. They call us Homo sapiens sapiens, or "twice-knowing human beings." What made the big difference was that we started having long conversations with each other. This is not necessarily a sign of great intelligence, as most of us now realize, but Homo sapiens sapiens, who began to appear about thirty to fifty thousand years ago, also displayed great powers of abstraction. As far as I can tell, that means we began thinking about things that weren't essential to everyday life. This ability led to what is now called civilization, a stage of evolution that appears to be in severe crisis.

Assuming that the genus "homo" survives at all, it will doubtless keep evolving; we can imagine that the next version of the species would look at its human ancestors as we now regard the apes, either patronizingly, or mildly amused with these "lowly animals." If any specimens still exist, we might even be put into zoos and studied. Maybe some future biologist will become famous for teaching one of us how to stop talking.

I don't want to get down on my species too much here. In fact, let it be known that I love my species very much—some members more than others, of course. But it *is* true that we are much too belligerent, and are currently breeding ourselves into a very tight corner. Nonetheless, in spite of all our mistakes and messes, we still think the world of ourselves.

Recently some humans have started accusing humanity of "species chauvanism," although they don't say we are "species chauvanist pigs," for obvious reasons. While I agree that we think too much of ourselves, it does seem only natural for any creature to be most concerned about the survival of its own kind. Anthropocentrism is no doubt as deeply programmed as any "ism" could possibly be.

Starting with my birth in 1942, we've now traced my origins back five million years to the birth of my species, so we might as well go all the way back to the moment just before the big bang, when you and I were living together, and, yes, we were very close. In fact, all of us were packed inside of one tiny little particle *smaller than an atom*. The astrophysicists call that place a singularity, but I think of it as the single mother of us all. Inside that particle were all of the billions of galaxies, the oceans and forests, cows and microbes, trucks, lawyers, pizzas, and dirty socks— everything packed in so tight that not even time could squeeze in. But everything was fine there, because everything was everything. Then some fool had a thought. The first thought was probably, "Hey, I exist! Check me out!" That distinction shattered the feeling of unity, causing this tiny particle to explode in a big bang that created space and time as it expanded, giving shape and substance to all the pieces of this gargantuan space-time universe. Finally, after fifteen or twenty billion years, this subatomic dance came up with me. I'm a long way from home, but I must say I'm looking pretty good these days, especially considering my age.

What has been overlooked is the irrational, the inconsistent, the droll, even the insane, which nature, inexhaustibly operative, implants in an individual, seemingly for her own amusement.

ALBERT EINSTEIN

My search for metaphysical sanity began in earnest sometime in early adolescence, and at age twelve I had what might have been my first revelation. I was spending a lot of time hanging out in the News and Tobacco Store on Norfolk's Main Street, reading the latest comic books and peeking into the girlie magazines whenever the proprietor wasn't looking. On that day, however, I was startled out of my routine by a face staring out at me from the cover of a magazine. For a few moments I stood transfixed, infused with a deep sense of calm that at the time I could not even begin to articulate. Only later in life, after years of studying world philosophy and practicing Buddhist meditation, did I realize that I had looked into the face of my first guru, Alfred E. Neuman.

Alfred E. is the young absurdist prince of the Western world, the great American tantric master, forever grinning at me and my generation from the cover of *Mad Magazine*.

His look is one of both detachment and bemusement as he watches over our mad, *Mad* world without concern, knowing that all is sham and fakery, and that this too shall pass. No matter what kind of cartoon apocalypse is going on around him—the whiz-bang-crash-kerplunk bonk-wham-barrrooom of falling empires and brutal wars and political summit meetings and important movie spectacles and significant fashion trends and increasing entropy—Alfred E. never stops grinning. And he never stops saying, "What, me worry?" This is the ultimate statement of cosmic realization. Even Lao Tzu, ancient China's greatest philosopher could not have said it better or more succinctly.

In some ways, I think my entire spiritual path has been an attempt to become more like Alfred E. Neuman; to be able to look at the world and grin just like he does. Many times, however, when I ask myself "What, me worry?" I find myself answering back, "Yes, me worry." Lately I've just been trying to grin like him. I figure that if I can master the grin, the mental state will follow.

> *Einstein pronounced the doom of continuous or*
> *"rational" space, and the way was made clear for*
> *Picasso and the Marx brothers and MAD.*
>
> MARSHALL MCLUHAN, *THE MEDIUM IS THE MESSAGE*

Maybe I identify so deeply with Alfred E. Neuman because my ears stick out just like his do. My mother used to try to console me by pointing out that Clark Gable had big ears too. I would answer sarcastically, "And don't forget Mickey Mouse."

In truth, my ears aren't so large, but they *are* situated quite low on my head, and therefore seem to stick out more. Some grade-school friends occasionally called me Dumbo, but one of my fraternity brothers in college was closer to the mark when he said to me, "If your ears were any lower, Wes, you'd have to use deodorant on them."

With ears like mine, *plus* being Jewish, I realized early that I would have to be clever if I was going to find a girlfriend in Norfolk, Nebraska. In my quest to get laid, I even tried to get my high-school buddies to start a rumor that Jewish circumcisions were specially crafted to make girls moan with pleasure. I hoped the girls would be overcome with curiosity. It didn't work. In fact, I didn't lose my virginity until college and the advent of long hair, which hid my ears.

Seriously, though, I doubt that my ears had all that much to do with my alienation. So what *did* cause it? Well, since the Buddha said that trying to figure out how your karma works will drive you crazy, I give up. How any of us got to be who we are is a big mystery. Western science searches for simple cause-and-effect relationships, but there are just too many variables. Centuries, millenia, lifetimes—who can fathom the forces that brought us to this moment? I subscribe to an old Tibetan Buddhist saying, "Roll all blames into one." We might as well just attribute everything to evolution, and try to move on.

During my high-school years, my parents began sending me to a Zionist summer camp in the piney woods of Wisconsin, hoping that I would meet other Jewish kids my age and discover my Jewish identity. It worked. The first few times we gathered at Camp Herzl's flag circle, I felt a secret thrill at the realization that everyone around me was Jewish. Not one of these kids believed that Jesus was the Messiah!

At Camp Herzl I became more comfortable with being Jewish, but I began to question my identity as an American. The camp counselors told us that our true home was in Israel, the land of milk and honey promised to our people in the Bible. Every day at camp we raised the Israeli flag and sang the Israeli national anthem, and our cabins were named after kibbutzim in Israel. Camp Herzl taught me that I belonged in the Middle East, not the Middle West.

Like most first- and second-generation American Jews, I was brought up to some degree in the cultural shadow of the European shtetl, a place of fear and sorrow where my people spoke the bastardized language, Yiddish. At Camp Herzl we were given a new image of what it meant to be a Jew. Our people weren't just cowering in musty synagogues, wailing and waiting for the messiah to come already; we were also pioneers and warriors, muscular and rugged, making the desert bloom. The Israelis had taken Hebrew, the tired old language of the Bible, and were using it to say, "Pass the salt, please." In Israel we even had our own Jewish army, praise the Lord!

I attended Camp Herzl every summer throughout high school and was a counselor there for a couple of summers during college. I found my Jewish identity, as my parents had hoped, but what they didn't count on, and wouldn't have known much about anyway, was that Camp Herzl would teach me about socialism.

The communal camp experience itself was a thrill for Norfolk's lone Jewish boy, what with everybody singing and eating together, and each group of cabinmates bonding like a tribe within a tribe. Meanwhile, we learned about the kibbutzim, the communal farms in Israel where people shared everything and lived as one big family. On a kibbutz there were theoretically no rich or poor members, and no competition for money or power; everyone worked and played together, united in a common goal. That sounded like a great idea to me at the time, and despite all the socialist experiments that have since failed, it still sounds like a good idea today. So call me a socialist, and blame it on Camp Herzl.

Socialism is indeed a part of Jewish heritage, being the brainchild of Industrial Age, European Jews who became labor leaders and intellectuals. I believe the socialist vision is a legacy the Jewish people should be proud to own; someday, we might yet regard Marx as highly as Moses.

When I was fifteen years old, I met a boy named Bobby Zimmerman at camp, but we didn't become friends. I won an award for being a good camper that year; Bobby always skipped his scheduled camp activities to hang out in the auditorium playing doo-wop songs on the piano for the girls. He was in a cabin of rowdy Duluth boys, known around the camp as "juvenile delinquents." After he became famous, a friend in Minneapolis sent me an old picture of Bobby Zimmerman at Camp Herzl, dressed in his white Sabbath clothes with the zipper of his pants undone. I gave the picture to the late rock promoter Bill Graham, who had it blown up into a billboard size to display at a concert featuring Bobby himself, now known as Bob Dylan.

GENERATION

gen·er·a·tion jen-ə-ˈrā-shən\ *n.*
1. the act or process of bringing into being 2. a) all the people born and living at about the same time b) a group of such people with some experience, belief, attitude, etc. in common 3. any of the stages of successive improvement in the development of a product, system, etc.

In the mid-1950s, a crack began to appear in the landscape of America, a crack that would eventually widen and deepen and split the nation apart—not North from South, or even so much liberal from conservative, but young from old. This rift would come to be known as the generation gap.

To some degree, each generation has a collective personality; who we become in life is strongly influenced by the dominant cultural milieu. For the most part, the parents of the baby boomers grew up in the lean and fearful period of the Great Depression, and then lived through the horrors of World War II. As a result, they were obsessed with security—

physical, financial, and political. Their children, on the other hand, were far more likely to have be born into relative affluence, their physical security and human rights guaranteed—at least if they were white and middle class. America was the world's new superpower superstar, and my generation's birthright included the promise of continued freedom and prosperity, as well as the opportunity to pursue any career, to reach any heights of achievement. Much to our parents chagrin, most of us decided to have a party first.

Perhaps *because* our future seemed relatively secure, many baby boomers felt free to get wild, to become juvenile delinquents, even, later, to drop out entirely. We saw our parents working too hard at jobs they didn't like, hanging onto deadened marriages, cautious about every penny they spent, stuck in perpetual planning and paranoia. They were "square," "uptight," "straight," and it was hard for us to understand their ways. If you already have sufficient money and freedom, we thought, then why worry about the future?

We grew up with great expectations, our fantasies shaped by the unbridled optimism that characterized America in the 1950s. Life was guaranteed to get bigger and better, more spectacular and more fun. As Robert Heilbroner says in his book *The Fifties*, that postwar decade saw the transformation of capitalism into consumerism. The newly powerful medium of television promoted not only products, but a basic belief in material goods as the key to happiness. Jesus may have said, "Give up all you own and follow me," but American free enterprise was saying, "Get everything you can and you will be among the blessed." Almost every advertisement, whether for Bendix carpet sweepers, Bayer asprin, or Buick automobiles, also sold the fantasy of the perfect family in their own home among many possessions, living happily ever after. Such great expectations could only lead to disappointment. Idealism slips too easily into cynicism.

At the same time, however, we were also constantly aware of a dark shadow on the horizon. Growing up with the atomic bomb almost literally hanging over our heads gave a fatalistic edge to our lives, and may have contributed to our restlessness and fascination with sex and danger. We might have understood, at least subconsciously, that the life we were facing was not as promising as it seemed in the advertisements.

All these factors figure in the development, sometime in the mid-fifties, of an American youth culture centered around images of rebels, and on rock-and-roll music. We kids were given the keys to the family car and drove around town blasting rock songs on the radio, all the while looking for the sex and excitement that this wild new music promised. "Oo-wee, oo-wee baby, oo-oo-wee..."

Those early rock-and-roll lyrics may have been pretty silly sometimes, but the music itself was immediate and visceral, pulling you into the moment and into your body. It was about sex and celebration, and very few of us could refuse the invitation to join the dance. That tribal beat was the first rumbling of a pagan revival, a bacchanal that would eventually shake the foundations of Judeo-Christian morality, leading to love-ins and nature worship and the new age. "Oo-wee, oo-wee baby, oo-oo-wee..."

In 1955, Bill Haley and the Comets enticed us to "Rock Around the Clock," and Bo Diddley, Buddy Holly, Chuck Berry, Little Richard, the Everly Brothers, the Coasters, and so many others sang out for us to shake our hips and fall in love. In 1956, approximately one half of Elvis Presley appeared on the *Ed Sullivan Show*, which only encouraged us kids to imagine what his other half was doing. Our parents were shocked by Elvis's wild sexual energy, and the media started calling him "Elvis the Pelvis." Later in the century, Reichians and other bioenergetic therapists would try to release even more of our culture's locked-up pelvic energy, energy that had started coming loose of its own accord in America's dancehalls in the '50s.

The rebel became the rage. Marlon Brando and James Dean captured the restless, defiant mood of young America in movies like *The Wild Ones* and *Rebel Without a Cause*. Fast cars and motorcycles also starred in those movies, giving young people new power and freedom and challenging us to see how far down the road and outside the law we could get. It was as if our nation's optimistic energy had sparked a corresponding restlessness in its youth, many of whom refused to accept either the institutional package of god-given truths and moral laws, or the pre-planned road to economic success. Our parents kept telling us how hard they had struggled and how good we had it, but we were beginning to feel how hollow a goal material wealth might be. We had to go out and prove something to ourselves on our own terms, to find our own morality and win our own respect and that of our peers, even if it meant delinquency and rootlessness.

> *...the hipster, the man who knows that if our collective condition is to live with instant death by atomic war...or with a slow death by conformity with every creative and rebellious instinct stifled, if the fate of twentieth-century man is to live with death from adolescence to premature senescence, why then the only life-giving answer is to accept the terms of death, to live with death as immediate danger, to divorce oneself from society, to exist without roots, to set out on that uncharted journey with the rebellious imperatives of the self.*
>
> NORMAN MAILER, "THE WHITE NEGRO"

Since I just didn't have the looks or character to affect that sullen and sinister James Dean-Marlon Brando attitude, my rebellion had to be one of laughter and scorn. I started paying closer attention to comedians and satirists like Steve Allen, Sid Ceasar, Ernie Kovacs, and, a little later, Lenny Bruce and Mort Sahl. With varying degrees of political savvy and bite, they showed me the underside of our consumer culture and the pretensions of its politicians and preachers. Since I had never felt entirely at home in American society, I loved hearing it ridiculed, and since I sensed that life itself was absurd, I identified with those who could laugh at it all, and make me laugh too.

I also read a lot of books during my high school and early college days. Being an early baby boomer, I was what you might call pre-post-literate. Many of us on the intellectual fringes of this rebellious youth culture were tantalized by romantic literary portraits of outsiders and nonconformists. J. D. Salinger, Herman Hesse, and James T. Farrell made rebels their heroes, even when they were tragic figures. I was also fascinated by the highly publicized real-life exploits of such authors such as F. Scott Fitzgerald, Ernest Hemingway, and Henry Miller. Their world seemed full of a kind of passion and intensity that could only be found on the edges of mainstream society.

This was not what my parents expected me to get out of my education. A college degree was supposed to be the baby boomer's ticket to respectibility and prosperity. What my parents, and many others like them, may not have counted on was this: A few good liberal-arts classes can lead you to doubt and question everything.

Nothing is more real than nothing.

SAMUEL BECKETT

Why do you not love yourself? Why do you love money? Why do you not embrace each other? That would be so simple.

FYODOR DOSTOYEVSKY, *THE IDIOT*

Since many of my friends from Camp Herzl lived in the Twin Cities, I decided to go to the University of Minnesota. I joined Sigma Alpha Mu, a Jewish fraternity which Bobby Zimmerman also pledged. He dropped out after refusing to recite the fraternal oath, but I went on to spend a couple of years in the fraternity social life, going to drinking parties and out to the big city restaurants, theaters, and nightclubs. I was acting out every rural boy's fantasy of being a sophisticated urbanite, a swinger, as they were called at the time. If the truth be known, I was trying to live according to the Playboy Philosophy.

The campus party scene soon began to bore me—perhaps because I wasn't a very good swinger—and by my junior year I had grown confused and depressed. I wasn't sure what I wanted to do when I graduated, but the life I was headed for looked suffocating. Since I wasn't good at science, and therefore not suited for medicine, I had simply assumed I would take the only other choice approved for young Jewish males, which is to say, law school. That would be followed inevitably by marriage, a nice house in the suburbs, a family, old age, and death. But what did it all mean in the end? And where was the romance and drama? What about the passionate life portrayed in my favorite books and movies? Young men throughout the ages have likely had such highly personal doubts. In the context of an emerging youth culture that was questioning *all* of America's institutions and values, however, my generation took these doubts to heart.

I was pulled toward the nascent counterculture by a wealth of influences, news of which traveled like subversive notes passed secretly between friends. One friend gave me Paul Goodman's book *Growing up Absurd*, another took me to see movies by Fellini and Godard. A whole group of us budding young radicals went to a Pete Seeger concert and sang along with his union-solidarity songs. One friend of mine started a campus newspaper called *The Gadfly*, whose masthead read, "Better to be a Socrates dissatisfied, than a pig satisfied."

In the early sixties, political protest was sweeping across America's college campuses. Civil rights, banning the bomb, and free speech were the main issues at first, although this began to change soon after President Kennedy was assassinated in 1963. When Lyndon Johnson took over and began escalating the war in Vietnam, many of us felt as though some kind of coup had taken place; that the American government no longer stood for freedom and justice. It no longer seemed to represent us.

> *We are people of this generation, bred in at least modest comfort, housed now in universities, looking uncomfortably to the world we inherit...Our*

work is guided by the sense that we may be the last generation in the experiment with living.

PORT HURON STATEMENT,
STUDENTS FOR A DEMOCRATIC SOCIETY, 1962

My own political disaffection was part of a much deeper turmoil. During my last two years in college I ran a constant metaphysical fever, delirious with doubt. Every humanities seminar I took exposed me to new revolutionary thinkers who blasted big, leaky holes in my universe of beliefs. Nietzsche showed me, in no uncertain terms, that my Judeo-Christian culture was built on fear and superstition. Karl Marx, whom I was assigned to read in a class on "the worldly philosophers," not only explained that capitalism is based on greed and competition, but detailed another, supposedly more humane way to organize society. To top that off, Sigmund Freud informed me that much of human behavior is governed by unconscious fears and desires, which, incidentally, helped explain a lot about capitalism.

Meanwhile, Albert Camus was telling me that the entire universe, including most of Western philosophy, was essentially absurd. I also read Joyce, Beckett, Gide, the Dadaists, and the beatniks. How could my tender young psyche remain whole or wholesome after all that? My parents may have thought college would mean upward mobility, but after four years I wanted nothing more than *outward* mobility. I wanted to get away from anything that smelled of the bourgeois. Later, I would come to want *inward* mobility even more.

We children of the future, how could we be at home in this today? We feel disfavor for all ideals that might lead one to feel at home even in this fragile, broken time of transition; as for its "realities," we do not believe that they will last. *The ice that still supports people today has become very thin; the wind that brings the thaw is blowing; we ourselves who are homeless constitute a force that breaks open ice and other all too thin "realities."*

FRIEDRICH NIETZSCHE, *THE GAY SCIENCE*

After a year-long college seminar on world religions, I began to see *all* beliefs and rituals as purely human inventions—often imaginative, yes, but certainly not connected to any absolute truth. From my sophisticated new existential promontory, some of my own people's practices suddenly seemed downright silly.

I wondered, for instance, who first told the Jews they should keep their heads covered as a sign of respect to Jehovah when they prayed? Imagine, way back in biblical times, some wild-eyed Jewish shaman wandering in from the desert and announcing, "Listen up everybody. I was just talking to God, and He says we should wear little hats on our head when we talk to Him." And everybody goes for it! Maybe the guy who supposedly heard this from God happened to own a haberdashery, and had a surplus of skullcaps to unload.

"And by the way," I can hear another Jewish shaman chiming in, "we should also start cutting off the skin at the end of every male child's penis so we can tell who belongs to our tribe and who doesn't." Oy vey! You'd think somebody would have objected. If, however, anyone did say, "Prophet or no prophet, this guy is meshuggenah and should maybe have his tongue cut out," no one listened.

I *do* remain in awe of the mighty combination of charisma and chutzpah that these early prophets must have needed to convince people of a god that you couldn't see! This was a great leap of mythic imagination, and it also proved to be an excellent means of social control: God is everywhere, and always knows what you are doing and thinking, so don't mess around or you *will* be punished. Big Father is watching you. Those Old Testament sages knew what they were doing. They had the right metaphors for their time, and the people who became their followers got the deity they needed and deserved.

Generation

GO OUT AND MAKE SOME OF YOUR OWN

23

Awe and respect notwithstanding, my entire adult spiritual search can be seen as a flight from Moses, the Confucius of the West. Raised with Dr. Spockian permissiveness, many of us rejected the moral imperatives of the Ten Commandments. We couldn't accept the idea that a jealous and wrathful God would punish us if we weren't good or didn't pray to Him alone. I still resent the fact that my religion tried to scare me into belief. It's simply not a good way to relate to the universe.

God's only excuse is that he does not exist.
FRIEDRICH NIETZSCHE

In my late-college metaphysical turmoil, I found solace and company with the existentialists. Even though their writing was often full of despair, they were still more fun to read than Kant and Descartes. The existentialists agreed with me that God was dead, and they echoed my own frustration at not being able to find any meaning to life. Somehow, this depersonalized the issue for me. It wasn't my fault that I couldn't find any good answers; it was simply the human condition.

What I found most fascinating, however, was that the existentialist thinkers saw the rational mind as part of the problem, *not* the solution. In fact, they mostly wanted out of their minds. As Nietzsche said, "I want, once and for all, *not* to know many things."

Back in the mid-nineteenth century, the existentialist philosophers and artists led the coup (off with their heads!) against Cartesian metaphysics. They stood Descartes on his head, saying, "I think, therefore I am not." The very act of thinking was what got in the way of being and, above all, the existentialists wanted to *be*. To be! That secular, anti-intellectual ideal would inform all subsequent Western art and philosophy, and become the cornerstone of the mid-century countercultures. It would stimulate broad interest in Eastern mysticism, with its emphasis on "non-doing" and "no-mind," and lead to the hippie be-in, which was nothing less than a joyous attempt to ritualize the existential ethos.

It is ironic that I labored through a three–year seminar in "Western thought"—a brow-twisting, mind-bending study of virtually all Western religions and philosophies—before finally coming to these iconoclastic thinkers, who told me it was all bunk and nonsense. If only I could have started with the existentialists when I was a freshman, I would have saved myself a lot of trouble and my parents a lot of money.

Being has not been given its due.

JEAN-PAUL SARTRE

Albert Camus was my favorite of the existentialists. I carried *The Myth of Sisyphus and Other Essays* around in my pocket for months, reading it over and over as if it were scripture. At the end of his own search for meaning, Camus had found absurdity, and he held it out like a banner, a secular challenge to the existential warrior: Can you live without god or meaning? I had no idea whether or not I could, but it seemed I would have to try. Angst a lot, Albert.

> *If I were a tree among trees, a cat among animals, this life would have a meaning, or rather this problem would not arise, for I should belong to this world. I should be this world to which I am now opposed by my whole consciousness and my whole insistence upon familiarity. This ridiculous reason is what sets me in opposition to all creation. I cannot cross it out with a stroke of the pen.*

ALBERT CAMUS

I sometimes wonder whether Camus would have taken up meditation practices had they been more accessible in his time. Eastern sages would agree with Camus's belief that "everything begins with lucid indifference," which sounds a lot like the "mindful equanimity" sought by Buddhists and Taoists. To be fully present and accepting of each moment was the existentialist's quest, but how does one do that? It's too bad Camus

Generation

couldn't find a way to quiet his thinking mind and calm his desperate need to know. It doesn't sound like he was having a very good time.

Our reason has driven all away. Alone at last, we end up by ruling over a desert.

ALBERT CAMUS

The summer after graduation, I took off on the obligatory tour of Europe, fully intending to come back to Minneapolis and attend law school in the fall, for lack of an alternative. First, though, I joined a vast torrent of American college kids pouring across the Atlantic. The first- and second-generation children of immigrants, freshly educated and newly rich, were all heading back to various mother countries to visit with their history. Or, as in my case, just to see the sights.

Although I enjoyed visiting the Eiffel Tower, the Tower of London, and Leaning Tower of Pisa, the towers did not thrill me as much as the erotic streets, the red-light districts and left banks, and especially those Parisian bohemian haunts like Montparnasse and the cafés Le Dome and La Rotonde—where my heros, Scott and Ernest, had bumped into Pablo and Gertrude and proceeded to set the style for a whole generation of American expatriots.

I remember trying to arrange perfect moments for myself, reading Sophocles on the steps of the Parthenon in the late afternoon light, or sitting with Rimbaud's poetry at a café in Paris, smoking Gitanes while surrounded by tables of artistes talking and drinking red wine. As I watched myself in these scenes, I would usually hear a voice in my head spinning out a narrative, a self-conscious account of the exciting bohemian life I was leading. The lost generation had made it seem so exciting to be lost, and I kept hoping to get lost in something.

One possibility for a heroic existence was offered to me in Israel. Despite having rejected Judaism, I still found it exciting to be in an entire country full of Jews. When I celebrated my first Sabbath in Tel Aviv, it suddenly occured to me that the whole country was observing it on Saturday rather than Sunday. Memories of Camp Herzl came back to me, along with the same feeling of belonging somewhere.

Finally, after agonizing indecision, I decided to postpone law school and stay in Israel for a year. I signed up for a nine-month student-work program at Kibbutz Ma'ayan Zvi, which I later found out was composed primarily of German Jews who had survived the Holocaust. Quite a number of the adults still had concentration–camp numbers tattooed on their arms, and my supervisor in the banana fields, who had been castrated by the Nazis, gave out his stern orders in a squeaky, high-pitched voice.

These kibbutzniks were still as much German as they were Israeli. They spoke Hebrew during the day and sang Israeli songs at mealtimes, but at night in their own living quarters, they spoke German and listened to Wagner on their phonographs. They were truly displaced persons.

While on the kibbutz, I fell in love with a Jewish girl from South Africa who had been kicked out of her country for antiapartheid activities. Like the German Jews, she couldn't return home, and had decided to make her life in Israel. That became an option for me as well. In Israel I could take part in building a nation for my ancestral people, and, in the process, just possibly help create a new socialist model for the world. It seemed a romantic enough notion for me. But fate, or karma, had different plans.

I was introduced to the next phase of my life one day in Jerusalem, when a friend, a Moroccan Jew from my kibbutz, turned me on to hashish. Walking around near the Wailing Wall, we were stunned by the historic implications of what we saw and choked with emotion. For two thousand years Jews had bowed their heads toward this ancient temple from afar, and now they were right in front of those holy old stones, touching them, kissing them. Looking around me that day, I thought I could remember being in Jerusalem before, in another lifetime. That is to say, I had a deja-Jew. Either some deep ancestral memory had been dredged up out of my DNA, or the hashish was talking.

I find it mildly ironic that I first got high in the holy city of Jerusalem, since drugs were an essential part of what led me farther away from Judaism and closer to the strange beliefs of beatniks and hippies, the lost tribes of America.

When I returned to Minneapolis in the summer of 1965, I found that many of my friends had begun hanging out around the blues bars and coffeehouses in the city's South Campus area. A new kind of energy was in the air, along with the smell of marijuana smoke. More and more disaffected youths were letting their hair grow long, organizing antiwar protests or art happenings, and getting excited about a revolution in politics and consciousness.

I immediately enrolled in graduate school at the University of Minnesota, partly to avoid the draft, but also to give myself time to figure out what I wanted to do with my life. I had a vague idea that I would go back and settle in Israel, but my allegiances quickly began to change.

That summer I fell in love with Karol, a stately, beautiful Jewess who had once been a runner-up Miss Minneapolis. Something else about her intrigued me as well: she had friends who were *real* Minneapolis hippies. We fueled our romance with marijuana and mushrooms, and were married the next year. We came to our prenuptial dinner high on marijuana, and I can still can see that sea of aunts and uncles' faces kissing and grinning at us like a scene from a Fellini movie.

Friends had introduced me to grass, but it was actually the U.S. government that first turned me on to LSD. The University of Minnesota Psychology Department, in a project funded by a government research grant, gave a few select graduate students 150-microgram doses of LSD, and then sat us down facing a wall that had been painted to look like an idyllic forest scene. The researcher stood behind us and asked questions about any changes we noticed in our perceptions. I remember that the wall didn't seem to change very much, but the researcher's voice gradually became more and more high pitched, until I finally had to be dismissed from the room because I was laughing so hard.

One of my next LSD trips started out fine, in a park in Minneapolis, but ended up as an archetypical "bummer." Three of us had ingested large doses and were down on the ground on all fours, pawing around in the dirt and growling. We flexed and unflexed our toes, trying to experience how our ape ancestors might have held on to tree limbs with their feet. I felt as though I could understand all of biological evolution from the inside out. Nowadays there are new age workshops that profess to "get you in touch with your animal nature," and even a process called "re-earthing," but this was long before all that.

We had a wonderful time playing in the park, but unfortunately we had arranged for a friend to come pick us up and drive us to see the Paul Butterfield Blues Band, who were playing on the top floor of Dayton's, a Minneapolis department store. As soon as we hit the downtown area I started to feel a little paranoid. It began as simple nervousness, no doubt triggered by the bombardment of urban stimuli, but soon turned into real fear. I became obsessed with the notion that I would see my aunt or some other relative and they would know I was stoned, I would be found out, exposed as the degenerate hippie that I was, and nobody in my family would ever speak to me again. Furthermore, no one in the world would ever hire me, or for that matter ever love me again. During previous psychedelic journeys I had been able to retain enough perspective on my thoughts to break out of such fear spirals, but this time it only grew worse.

I didn't want to tell my friends that I was freaking out, but things kept getting worse for me. We arrived at Dayton's without incident, but on our way up to the concert, the elevator stopped on the third floor. When the doors opened, a cop was standing right there. I was certain he knew I was high. Then he got in the elevator with us. My internal freakout became uncontrollable—the ride up to the tenth floor took an eternity, and by the time we got there I was petrified with fear of everything.

My friends got me home and fed me some Thorazine, and I awoke feeling all right the next morning. But I will never forget how that spiral of fear fed on itself, in what felt like a brush with true insanity.

Of course there were good LSD trips too, usually taken in controlled settings, where I could direct my attention inward. On a few of these journeys I felt as if I was in contact with ultimate reality, experiencing everything as part of an inseparable unity, perfect in and of itself. There were also times when a great surge of love and appreciation for the world would rise in me, leaving me with a deep sense of peace. Later in life, I found similar experiences and insights through Buddhist meditation, in the context of an ancient and highly articulated metaphysical practice. I feel very privileged to have been offered of both these ways to examine the nature of reality, and learn how to love it.

On October 6th, 1966, LSD became illegal. In San Francisco that event was publicized with the following "Prophecy of a Declaration of Independence":

> *When in the flow of human events it becomes necessary for the people to cease to recognize the obsolete social patterns which had isolated man from his consciousness and to create with the youthful energies of the world revolutionary communities to which the two–billion–year old life process entitles them, a decent respect to the opinions of mankind should declare the causes which impel them to this creation.*
>
> *We hold these experiences to be self–evident, that all is equal, that the creation endows us with certain inalienable rights, that among these are: the freedom of the body, the pursuit of joy, and the expansion of consciousness, and that to secure these rights, we the citizens of this earth declare our love and compassion for all conflicting hate-carrying men and women of the world.*

In many ways, I feel lucky to have been born early in the baby boom, to have grown up as America was becoming a big, rich superpower. Most of my friends will agree that we had it good. We were given, if not the fountain of youth itself, at least a decade-long extension of our adolescence. It's as though our parents told us, "Take the '60s off, kids. Have fun, but be back by 1973." So many people I know spent countless years in graduate school, traveled the world, tried on various careers and lifestyles, and survived for the most part on the fringes of this affluent society with very little money. After all, when it ran out, many of us could just send home for more.

At the time, however, my life seemed quite difficult and confusing. I changed my graduate-school major four times and attended three different graduate schools between 1965 and 1967. Although I was eager to forge ahead with some sort of career plan, nothing seemed to fit—maybe because all the real action was in the growing counterculture. What could compete with the chance to transform the world, or to be part of a whole new style of bohemia? Meanwhile, there was one constant limitation to my freedom of choice: I had to stay in graduate school in order to avoid the draft. My bottom line was staying out of Vietnam.

Finally, in the spring of 1967, I could not tolerate another college seminar. After rejecting the option of shooting myself in the foot, I decided to see a shrink at the University of Minnesota and fake a psychosis. I was hoping to get a letter saying I was crazy and therefore unfit for military service. The university assigned me to a psychologist whose name, believe it or not, was Dr. Dredge. Luckily, I really didn't need therapy, just somebody I could fool into *thinking* I needed therapy. Dr. Dredge was my man.

I came into our first meeting with my head bowed, looking really sad, my hands shaking badly enough that I could pretend to be embarrassed by their twitches. Occasionally I would jerk my head up with a startled look, as if I had suddenly been reminded of something unpleasant.

Dr. Dredge watched this show with pity. I told him that my symptoms were due to the fact that I had taken several bad acid trips, and that my latest one included a vision in which the entire earth had become a bed of quicksand. Even worse, this vision kept returning without warning; sometimes while walking along, I would suddenly be afraid to take another step. Dr. Dredge had heard about LSD flashbacks and was sympathetic. After about five sessions he agreed to write a letter saying that I was too crazy to kill. Uncle Sam believed him, and soon the mail brought me the magic classification, 4F.

Having successfully dodged the draft meant that I could stay home and struggle against racism and imperialism in America, or, as many of us would have called it, the belly of the beast. A few months later, Karol and I headed for California, where we heard that the hippies were really hip and the revolution had already happened.

BEATIFICATION

Chapter Three

No one ever really chooses a subculture. The style that any given rebellion takes is a simply a matter of timing, or karma, if you will. My birthdate placed me on the cusp of two subcultures, and I see myself as a kind of mongrel bohemian, with a beatnik head and a hippie heart. Although I would have loved to have joined up with the beatniks, I came along too late to make the scene. When I got to San Francisco, I was assigned to the hippies instead.

Back in the early 1960s, anyone listening for the sound of a different drummer as I was, might have heard a bongo drum. It would have been growing fainter to be sure, beginning to be drowned out by folk-rock music (electric guitars were just tuning up in the Haight-Ashbury), but there was at least one bongo still being beaten in a pad in San Francisco's North Beach by some mustachioed guy in dark sunglasses, a guy so cool you could hardly see him. At least that was the essential beatnik image, and it seemed inviting to many of us restless young Americans, even if we didn't understand what was really going on behind the glasses.

The beats had come of age in the fifties, reacting against the post-war era's social conformity. They were, as Allen Ginsberg once said, "beatifically beat down." In other words, they were spiritual outcasts, driven into cellars and coffeehouses by the harsh light of American optimism and the forward rush of progress. The beat costume was old denim, working- class clothing, black sweaters, and the everpresent sunglasses through which to view the world darkly. The punks and hip-hoppers would later return to some of these darker beatnik styles, after the colorful hippie flower children had dragged bohemia out of the shadows for a brief moment in the sun.

The beat poets were existentialists, but with a distinctly American flavor, streetwise and anti-intellectual. Unlike the Europeans, the beats were not just thinking about existentialism, they were trying to live it, to be fully alive for every note in the swirling riff of life. They wanted a never-ending series of perfect moments, or, to use the word they adopted from Japanese Zen, *satori*: That's the ultimate in hipness; when you get permanently "with it."

The beat generation turned to the East for metaphysical sustenance, specifically to Zen Buddhism, which seemed hidden and mysterious like themselves. Zen, after all, is a radical form of cool—not just worldy cool, but cosmic cool. Cool even in the face of death. Zen also has an edge of irony that suited the beats perfectly. And since poetry was their chosen medium, the beats were fascinated with Zen's mind-twisting koans and haikus of sudden ordinariness.

Out of that pack of characters known as the beat generation, Jack Kerouac, Ginsberg, and Gary Snyder became my heros and mentors, and remain such to this day. They wrote political manifestoes I could salute, and spiritual verses I could bow down to. It was mainly through them, as well as Alan Watts and a few others, that I became fascinated with Buddhist and Hindu ideas. The beat writers introduced exotic words like karma, dharma, nirvana, and mantra into the hipster's lexicon and, although I only had a vague idea what they meant, I was eager to learn.

Kerouac had first captured and opened my heart back in college. I've reread him again and again, and am still moved by his aching attempt to love the world, in spite of all the suffering he saw. I felt his dilemma to be my own, just as I had felt Camus's to be, but Kerouac was a generation closer to me, working in the fresh milieu of American cultural experimentation.

Kerouac was the American Joyce, with complete access to his melodious flow of mind, spilling and singing out jazz-inspired colloquial prose that spoke to a generation just beginning to experience other rhythms. More importantly, Kerouac awakened us to the possibility of personal freedom and revelation. He translated Buddhist words and concepts into an American idiom, turning the highway into a spiritual path. Just reading him was enough to make me want to jump in a car and head for a farther shore, wherever that might be, in search of "the golden eternity." Many would follow in Kerouac's tracks, and, as early as 1958, he prophecied what the hippie saga would look like:

> I've been reading Whitman, know what he says, "Cheer up slaves, and horrify foreign despots," he means that's the attitude for the Bard, the Zen Lunacy bard of old desert paths, see the whole thing is a world full of rucksack wanderers, Dharma Bums refusing to subscribe to the general demand that they consume production and therefore have to work for the privilege of consuming, all that crap they didn't really want anyway such as refrigerators, TV sets, cars, at least new fancy cars, certain hair oils and deodorants and general junk you finally always see a week later in the garbage anyway, all of them imprisoned in a system of work, produce, consume, work, produce, consume, I see a vision of a great rucksack revolution, thousands or even millions of young Americans wandering around with

rucksacks, going up to mountains to pray, making children laugh and old men glad, making young girls happy and old girls happier, all of 'em Zen Lunatics who go about writing poems that happen to appear in their heads for no reason and also by being kind and also by strange unexpected acts keep giving visions of eternal freedom to everybody and to all living creatures...

JACK KEROAUC, *DHARMA BUMS*

Although I didn't really encounter his work until later in the 1960s, Gary Snyder had a powerful influence on my understanding of the world, and of what would be required if we were to change its course. Of that small beat literary crowd, he was the one who took meditation most seriously, and in the middle of the hoopla he disappeared in Japan for almost a decade to study Zen. Upon his return he started a Zen center in the Sierra foothills, and in 1969 published *Earth House Hold*, subtitled, "Technical Notes and Queries to Fellow Dharma Revolutionaries." In this book, which became very popular in the San Francisco counterculture, Snyder described how personal and political transformation were the same good work. He also brought together Native American and Zen Buddhist views of the natural world, and in doing so began to lay down a metaphysical context for the coming environmental movement.

As a poet I hold the most archaic values on earth. They go back to the late Paleolithic: the fertility of the soil, the magic of animals, the power-vision in solitude, the terrifying initiation and re-birth, the love and ecstasy of the dance, the common work of the tribe. I try to hold both history and wilderness in mind, that my poems may approach the true measure of things and stand against the unbalance and ignorance of our times.

GARY SNYDER, *THE SOUTHERN REVIEW*

Although he's been appearing in coat and tie since the 1980s, Allen Ginsberg is etched in my memory sitting on an open-air stage, beard flowing and beads jangling, his harmonium droning while he intones a mantra to exorcise America's demonic ignorance and greed. In fact, Ginsberg may have done as much as any of his fellow beatniks to bring Hindu and Buddhist culture to the West simply by chanting "om" at countless protests and demonstrations from the 1960s onward.

Ginsberg's poem "Howl" left me stunned, filled with a mixture of hope and fear. The consummate mythopoetic indictment, it denounced the gods of war and commerce. In calling our civilization "Moloch," Ginsberg named the evil and threw down the gauntlet:

> Moloch! Solitude! Filth! Ugliness! Ashcans and un-
> obtainable dollars! Children screaming under
> the stairways! Boys sobbing in armies! Old
> men weeping in the parks!
> Moloch! Moloch! Nightmare of Moloch! Moloch
> the loveless! Mental Moloch! Moloch the heavy
> judger of men!
> Moloch the incomprehensible prison! Moloch the
> crossbone soulless jailhouse and congress of
> sorrows! Moloch whose buildings are judg-
> ment! Moloch the vast stone of war! Moloch
> the stunned governments!
> Moloch whose mind is pure machinery! Moloch
> whose blood is running money! Moloch whose
> fingers are ten armies! Moloch whose breast is
> a cannibal dynamo! Moloch whose ear is a
> smoking tomb!

Ginsberg wrote those words in 1956. Ten years later, his Moloch had become the Vietnam War, and Ginsberg an elder spokesperson for the antiwar movement and the hippies. Once he even suggested that everyone over the age of fourteen take acid, "including the President and our vast hordes of generals, executives, judges, and legislators of these States. {They should} go to nature, find a kindly teacher or Indian Peyote chief or guru guide, and assay their consciousness with LSD."

The beat poets confronted a latter-day version of the same industrial civilization that had once been opposed by William Blake and the Romantics, as well as Thoreau and Whitman and the Transcendentalists, all of whom the beats drew on for inspiration. They answered the same call to love and celebrate life, in contrast to mainstream society's attempt to conquer and control it. The beats, and the hippies who followed them, were attempting to stage a spiritual revival in America, to start something life-affirming in these perpetual last days of Western civilization.

Beatniks and hippies were neo-pagans, seeking reconnection with the body, the natural world, and the cosmic cycles (What's your sign?). Drawing on all manner of world cultures, they became mythological collage artists. The beats and hippies were in recovery from monotheism. They were polytheistically perverse.

Of course many people joined one or the other of these movements just for kicks, but others were after bona fide postindustrial, neoshamanic visions, and they got them—through drugs and breathwork and sweatlodges and meditation and jazz and rock-and-roll. Often, their visions included the message that humankind was off balance and out of control, that our survival instinct needed a tuneup and readjustment, and, furthermore, that it might be time to come up with some new stories about how to live.

The beats and hippies tried to write these stories; that is, to shape a world that did not revolve around competition and individualism, property and war. Their goal was to move from the future back to the present, from solemnity to celebration, from speed and greed to slow down and share, from the objective to the subjective, and, at the same time, from the individual back to the collective or tribe.

> *Who knows, my God, but that the universe is not one vast sea of compassion actually, the veritable holy honey, beneath all this show of personality and cruelty.*

> JACK KEROUAC

HIPPIFICATION

Chapter Four

After one more chorus, he presses his guitar up against his stack of amplifiers, feedback screaming, and dry-humps the back of the guitar. He slips out of the strap and drops to his knees, the guitar flat on the stage, and sprays lighter fluid over the face of the instrument. Bending down, he gives the guitar one quick kiss goodbye and ignites the fluid. Flames dance in front of him. His fingers flutter encouragement. He grabs the flaming Fender by the neck and breaks it apart on the stage, swinging it wildly. The pieces are discarded—burnt offerings—into the audience as he staggers off the stage and into history. Jimi Hendrix has played the Monterey Pop Festival.

JOEL SELVIN, *MONTEREY POP*

In June of 1967, six of us piled into Stephen Kaplan's mother's big Buick and left Minneapolis for California to attend the Monterey Pop Festival, the first of the great counterculture rock-and-roll celebrations. Stephen had started publishing an alternative pop-culture magazine called *Twin Beat*, a sort of midwestern *Rolling Stone*, and he wanted to do a story on the festival. Everyone else just came along for the ride, which turned out to be a typical maniacal 1960s road adventure, with all of us stoned and laughing our way across Route 80 toward the magical land of California, the place that my hero Kerouac, the godfather of road trips, had called "the end of the land sadness, end of the world gladness."

As soon as we pulled into Monterey, we became ecstatic. The city was swarming with young people, many of them wearing swirling psychedelic tie-dyes, the multicolored flag of hippiedom. Others were dressed up as cowboys or Indians or Edwardian ladies and gentlemen or whoever else they wanted to be at the moment. We saw people laughing in cars, dancing in the streets, and flipping peace signs to everyone who passed. The Beatles had just come out with *Sergeant Pepper's Lonely Hearts Club Band*, and everywhere you went, carloads of hippies had their windows rolled down and their radios blasting out the title song, everyone singing along as loud as they could. We were a true subculture. We were a force to be reckoned with. "We hope you will enjoy the show..."

A giant Buddha had been erected opposite the main entrance to the Monterey Fairgrounds, and every concertgoer was given an orchid as they entered (100,000 orchids had been flown in from Hawaii for the event). The festival's theme was "Peace, Love and Flowers." The unnamed ingredient in the theme was "Drugs." For three whole days, the marijuana smoke at the fairgrounds was thicker than the morning fog, and if you looked deeply into a passerby's eyes, which you often did, you would like as not meet dilated pupils and that dazed-amazed look of someone who has just landed on another planet.

Even with all the drugs, however, there were hardly any arrests that weekend, probably because the police assigned to the event were continually being kissed by the hippie girls. By the end of the festival, most of the officers were wearing flowers in their hats or on their gun belts.

From the very first day, a rumor had been spreading that the Beatles were going to make a surprise appearance. Whenever a helicopter flew over the stadium people would shout, "It's the Beatles! They're here!" On the last night, the excitement mounted as the Mamas and Papas, the final scheduled act, took the stage. The evening had begun with Janis Joplin, tearing up the crowd with her version of "Ball and Chain," followed by a still relatively unknown British band called The Who, who closed with a song called "My Generation," and then shocked the audience by smashing up their instruments right there on stage. Then came that legendary Jimi Hendrix performance in which he burned his guitar during his final number, a scorching, screeching version of "Wild Thing." The Mamas and Papas had to follow all that with their folk-pop ballads, but they did all right anyway, and had the crowd singing and swaying along with "California Dreamin'." Still, everybody was waiting for the Beatles! We were Sergeant Pepper's Lonely Hearts Club Band, and they were our leaders.

Finally, after the second encore, Papa John Phillips stepped up to the microphone and said he had a very special announcement to make. The crowd gasped as he continued, "I have the great pleasure of presenting a very special guest here in Monterey tonight. Everybody please give a warm welcome for..." By now the crowd was screaming so loud we could barely hear Phillips finish his sentence, "...Scott MacKenzie, here to sing his hit song, 'If You're Goin' to San Francisco, Be Sure to Wear Some Flowers In Your Hair!'"

Most of us sang along with MacKenzie's hippie anthem, but, as we used to say, *what a bring down.*

In Terry Southern's book, *Red Dirt Marijuana*, a black farmhand named K.C. tells the twelve-year-old Harold about marijuana and why it is against the law to smoke it, saying, "It's cause a man *see* too much when he get high. I tell you they's a lotta trickin' an lyin' go on in the world—they's a lotta ole *bull-crap* go on in the world—well, a man git high, he see right through all them tricks an' lies, an' all that ole bull-crap. He see right through there into the *truth* of it!"

"Truth of what?" asks the boy.

"Ever'thing," replies K.C.

We didn't need marijuana to see through all the ole bull-crap in America back in the 1960s, but it may have eased the nausea that seeing through it induced. To start with, our parents and teachers rarely talked about the fact that our nation was built on top of other people's bones, or that 60 million buffalo had been slaughtered in less than one hundred years as our immigrant ancestors "settled" the continent. My generation at least knew something about the unspeakable crimes of slavery, but was just awakening to the ongoing racism in all areas of American life. And, most damning of all, every day on the television news, we watched our government intensify a war against a tiny peasant nation halfway around the planet, dropping unimaginable numbers of bombs on them, burning down their villages and jungles.

My parents were blind to these atrocities. Perhaps they were too deeply scarred by the recent horrors in Europe to question the country that had given them refuge. In America, after all, they were finally enjoying security and freedom, especially in comparison to places like Moscow and Dachau, so they didn't want to rock the boat. And they didn't want their kids to rock it either, let alone to roll it over.

For a while in the 1960s and 1970s, I felt completely estranged from my biological family. I was a radical and an atheist. I had my astrological chart read, did gestalt therapy, in which I beat up a pillow that represented my mother, and, of course, I wore my hair long. Whenever I went back to Norfolk for a visit, as I did on the way back from Monterey, my mother would shake her head in disbelief and say, "When are you going to do something about that hair?" The other thing she often said was, "When are you going to become staple?" She meant "stable," of course, but it always made me imagine myself as a paper cutout, actually stapled down somewhere. I shuddered to think of it.

Instead, inspired by the huge tribe of hippies I'd seen in California, I let my hair grow even longer. I wanted to join up full-time with this amorphous band of visionaries and thrill-seekers, and long hair was the unmistakable badge of membership. Soon after our return from Monterey, Karol and I left Minneapolis for good and moved to San Francisco.

My blood relatives and my nation didn't understand me. I left home and joined a generation.

The spiritual revolution will be manifest and proven. In unity we shall shower the country with waves of ecstasy and purification. Fear will be washed away; ignorance will be exposed to sunlight; profits and empire will lie drying on deserted beaches...

THE SAN FRANCISCO ORACLE, 1967,
PROMOTING THE FIRST HUMAN BE-IN,
THE FIRST GREAT INGATHERING OF THE HIPPIE TRIBES

The late sixties were an explosive moment in history. Youth rebellions took place all across America, as well as in Mexico City, London, and Paris. A common cry went up from our generation's new, electronically connected consciousness, demanding freedom and justice for all, and an end to war. San Francisco was the metaphysical heart of the rebellion.

To Karol and me, the city seemed like Jerusalem and Babylon rolled into one. This was the headquarters of the Aquarian Age, as well as a sensual, fun-loving town. Exotic Asian and Latin American influences spiced the culture and the food, and the next outrageous experiment in art and/or life was always just around the corner. This was the far edge of the continent, the farthest edge of Western civilization. It felt like home.

This is a city that has always welcomed aliens. Separated from the rest of the continent by the San Francisco Bay, it sits alone on its own peninsula, aloof and somewhat at sea on an isolated strip of land shaped something like a California Grey Whale. You can imagine it stretched out, its head resting in the waters where the Pacific Ocean meets the Bay so that its forehead anchors one end of the Golden Gate Bridge. The neighborhood of North Beach sits right where the blowhole would be, ready to shoot subterranean beatnik-Italian rebel juices up through the nozzle of old Coit Tower, right up into the big winds blowing in from the Pacific, winds that might carry them onto the continent to seed the dry crusted ground of America and inspire something different to grow there.

Even today, visitors can sense that just beneath the surface of this serious Pacific Rim financial center and all-American city is a vital core of otherness, an ever-evolving anarchist convention and costume party filled with jesters and fools and misplaced out-of-time geniuses, each with their own unique mix of sexual, spiritual, and political identities. Although the city has been called a backwater by East Coast snobs and L.A. slicks, locals know that the new paradigm is always spawning somewhere out there in the Bay. So come on out folks and we'll tell you in person what we have in mind for the next millennium.

In 1967, San Francisco was still relatively small. There was hardly ever a traffic jam on the freeways or a wait at the bridges' toll plazas, even during rush hour; the Transamerica Pyramid, the four towering Embarcaderos, the fifty-two–story Bank of America building, and most of the other steel-and-glass skyscrapers that now dominate the skyline had not yet been built. But the oldtimers were already bemoaning the city's ruination, telling us newcomers stories about the good ol' days of the '30s, '40s, or even '50s. On September 24th, 1967, just a few months after my arrival, venerable *San Francisco Chronicle* columnist Herb Caen wrote, "How to tell the kids of today about the glories of the bridgeless bay and the curving beauty of the ferryboats? The steam train that curlicued its way to the top of Tamalpais? The pasta at Papa Coppa's? Benny Goodman came to McFadden's Ballroom in Oakland, and I haven't heard a more exhilarating sound before or since, and that goes for the Rolling Stones."

Every generation can work up nostalgia for its past, and San Franciscans are especially prone to rapsodizing over bygone glories—the wild, lawless days of the Gold Rush, the hopped-up excitement of the jazz age, or the mystical experimentations of the beatnik era. It is, however, also true that things have changed dramatically since mid-century. As the region's population skyrocketed, concrete pavement and housing tracts began to take over the rolling hills, while landfill consumed the waters of the Bay itself.

In 1978, Malcolm Margolin, a bearded hippie Jew from the East Coast, published a wondrous book called the *Ohlone Way* (after the name of native tribes of the region) about the Bay Area and Northern California before white people came. Suddenly we began to understand what had been lost in the building of this great city and its suburbs, and some of us became nostalgic for a time we'd never experienced.

Margolin used diaries and dispatches from missionaries, military men, and adventurers to present a picture of what the first Europeans found in the San Francisco Bay region. In 1700, the bay itself was a full third larger than it is today, and teeming with life. Great pods of whales often swam right into the Bay, and herds of sea lions were so enormous that one missionary said they sometimes covered the entire surface of the water "like a pavement." Thousands of acres of fresh and saltwater swamps (of which only 5 percent remain) surrounded the Bay, attracting an amazing array of marine and bird life, including huge flocks of geese, ducks, pelicans, herons and other seabirds. According to Margolin, "Ducks were so thick that one European hunter told how several were frequently killed with one shot, " and, according to missionary Father Juan Crespi, the geese that wintered in the Bay were "uncountable." Just a few ducks and geese remain these days, and they usually look a bit lost.

The hills that surround the Bay, now given over to housing developments, were covered with forests of redwood, oak, and bay trees, broken by fields of tall native grasses grazed by great herds of elk and antelope. Coyotes, bobcats, mountain lions, foxes, wolves, and bears roamed these hills, while bald eagles and giant condors glided overhead. In the 1700s, a French sea captain named La Perouse wrote, "There is not any place in the world which more abounds in fish and game of every description... inexpressible fertility."

Reading Margolin's book, I was saddened, frightened, and angered. Change is inevitable, but our civilization seemed largely oblivious to its impact on the rest of nature. Most academics didn't seem to notice the problem, government officials were sensitive only to the concerns of those who could vote, and the general population was largely unaware of environmental issues. Back in the late '60s and early '70s, it was primarily counterculture types, with their nature worship and anticonsumer stance, their emphasis on sharing and simple living, who tried to address the imbalance.

Today biologists are raising California condors in captivity, in an attempt to save them from extinction. The bald eagle, symbol of a proud young nation, is also an endangered species, while the grizzly bear, California's totem animal, can no longer be found in the Golden State. Something has gone terribly wrong. One of the fundamental beat and hippie indictments against America was for its crimes against nature. And while we couldn't go back to native ways, it was becoming apparent that we had to change our own.

Chapter Five

48

Humor and satire are the outsider's best tools. That, along with the fact that suffering is good mulch for humor, may explain why there are so many Jewish comedians. As a child, I used humor to get around my parents, and to distance myself from a culture I didn't belong to. As I grew up, I found even better reasons to make fun of society, and by the time I came to San Francisco I had mustered the courage to go public.

A few months after we arrived, I got myself a regular weekend gig at a North Beach coffeehouse, singing some Tom Lehrish songs I had written, accompanying myself on an electrified ukulele. I was sort of a political Tiny Tim. Most of my barbs were aimed at the government, but I did some jokes about Zen Buddhism, as well as hippie jargon and behavior. One of my songs was entitled "My Thing Is Your Thing and Everything Is Everything."

My wife, Karol, would pass the hat after each of my sets, and we usually made enough to survive until the next weekend. We didn't need much. At the time we were living in a beautiful Victorian mansion on

California and Franklin streets that had once housed the M.J.B. coffee dynasty, but was now a hippie commune. Although we never worried about money, we did have some very lean days. When Dave "Snaker" Ray brought his band out from Minneapolis to audition for legendary rock promoter Bill Graham at the Fillmore Ballroom, the whole group stayed with us. The band was completely broke, and for many days we all lived on a big pot of soup made from chicken necks, the only part of the bird we could afford. Still, it *was* chicken soup. What more does a Jewish boy need?

I began going to improvization workshops at the San Francisco Committee, a satirical theater group modeled after Chicago's Second City. Soon I had the chance to audition for the San Francisco Mime Troupe and was accepted. One night, as I was preparing for my first Mime Troupe show, I turned on the radio and heard a disc jockey reading the days top news stories on KSAN-FM, a new underground station. His presentation struck me as much too bland for a counterculture audience.

Within a few days, I had decided to go see KSAN's program director, "Big Daddy" Tom Donahue—a heavy in every sense of the word. I suggested to him that his DJs shouldn't just tear the same old wire copy off the UPI teletype machine and read the headlines. I thought that KSAN should present the news in a way that was satirical, politically subversive, and somehow psychedelic. I was shocked and a little frightened when Big Daddy replied, in his booming bass voice, "Okay, you come in and try it out. You do the news tomorrow on KSAN."

After a month or so of experimenting, Donahue hired me to be KSAN's news director. So I gave up my chance to be a Mime Troupe actor in order to become a radical hippie broadcaster, fomenting revolution and eventually helping to make a tidy profit for KSAN and its corporate owner, Metromedia.

When people talk about the golden age of radio they usually mean the 1930s and 1940s, when America's best actors and writers were producing radio theater, and the inimitable voices of Jack Benny, Fred Allen, and

Arthur Godfrey growled across the nation's airwaves. But in the late 1960s and early 1970s, even though television was by then the dominant medium, another brief golden age took place, this time on the FM dial.

The difference between AM and FM has to do with how the air is modulated into a signal or, literally, how the air waves. AM stands for amplitude modulation, FM for frequency modulation. Or, as we used to say, "FM broadcasters do it with frequency." Since FM has a wider dynamic range than AM, we also have better high ends and low ends. And that was certainly the case in the early days of FM rock-and-roll.

Before 1967, the FM band was used mostly for classical music, with a few jazz, foreign-language, and religious stations scattered up and down the dial. Since very few radios were even fitted to receive the signal, there was little money to be made or lost in FM, which also meant more room for experimentation.

FM finally came alive when rock-and-roll music began to move from the Top 40 AM stations over to FM. This coincided with the shift from 45 rpm pop-music singles to albums, and the simultaneous explosion of the Sixties counterculture. The hippies were becoming a substantial marketing demographic, and we wanted to hear our music in the highest fidelity possible, programmed for us by members of our own tribe. I happened to be in the right place at the right time. The now-legendary KSAN, or "Jive 95" as we tagged it, was the premier FM rock-and-roll station in the country.

For a few years before the profiteers took over, KSAN and stations like it across the nation were rightfully termed "underground radio." We promoted antigovernment protests, we savagely criticized the president and congress, we preached against capitalism and the Judeo-Christian religions, we openly encouraged the use of marijuana and LSD, and, of course, we played the music to accompany all these activities. We were truly tribal radio, filling the heads of American youth with a call to sex, drugs, rock-and-roll, and revolution.

KSAN was great radio theater. The disc jockeys had names like Reno Nevada, Dusty Street, Voco, and Edward Bear. Tony Bigg, formerly an

AM disc jockey, changed his name to Tony Pigg when he got a job at KSAN. Tony gave me my "radio name," Scoop, the day I broke a story in San Francisco that the Chicago Eight's defense team was planning to call Allen Ginsberg to the witness stand. The nickname has stuck with me ever since. When people look puzzled by it, I tell them my parents were in ice cream.

At the time, our radio names didn't seem pretentious at all. Everybody around us was playing with their identities, dressing up and, trying to trip one another out. We wanted to become new people, children of the future, born again in the Age of Aquarius.

Listening to tapes from those days, it amazes me that KSAN was allowed to continue broadcasting. The fact that the government did not shut us down is either a testament to the power of the First Amendment, or to the inefficiency of the FCC and FBI. It could also be that we weren't that important to anybody but ourselves.

I was KSAN's news director from 1968 through 1970, and continued doing weekly features and documentaries for the station (between trips to Asia) until 1979. In my early years as news director, I was usually the entire news department as well, which meant gathering news, writing it, making it up, splicing tape together, and doing the announcing. As was the case for most people in the underground media back then, my work was my play. I was committed to some vague idea of revolution, but I was also having a good time living out my bohemian-artist fantasies.

My deepest and most urgent political commitment was to stop the Vietnam War. Beyond that, I held an almost mystical idea of a peace-loving society, one where people lived without envy or competition, exploring consciousness and creativity, and joyously sharing the planet with all living things. This was the classic hippie vision, infused with a spiritual longing; our version of the American Dream.

My work at KSAN gradually made me into a radical, or, at the very least, a sympathizer. Anyway, I played the part, swept along by the political turmoil and excitement. And at times it went way beyond mere reporting. The KSAN news department functioned as a communication center for the antiwar movement, the Black Panthers, and even the Weather Underground. Being a radical was part of my job description. While my first news broadcasts were mostly satirical, I soon turned to serious calls for activism and protest. I began to sign off my program with, "If you don't like the news, go out and make some of your own."

Although my newscasts and features became a central element of KSAN's programming, the main message remained the music. Hippies and radicals alike were caught up in the spell of the new rock-and-roll, the heartbeat of our common generational revolt. Whenever authorities tried to squelch political protest, we told each other that at least "they can't bust our music," meaning that we would always be able to get messages of flower power and revolution to "the people" through song. How wonderfully innocent we were. "T-t-t-talking 'bout my generation."

This golden age of counterculture radio was largely the result of freeform programming, a format in which disc jockeys were able to create their own shows. They did just that at KSAN, sampling from all the world's music in sublime segues and sets of sounds that took listeners on soaring, imaginative musical flights. Considering that the musicians who made the music, the DJs who programmed it, and the listeners who heard it were often equally stoned, it's little wonder that moments of deep communion and connection occured, imprinting KSAN on the minds of its loyal audience. Back in those days you would sometimes be moved to cry out loud to your radio, "Oh wow!"

I remember Edward Bear, one freeform night on KSAN, playing a Buffalo Springfield tune that segued into a Mozart sonata, which he then mixed in and out of a Balinese gamelon piece—the counterpoints cross-culturally counterpointing with each other—and then resolved the whole set with some blues from John Lee Hooker.

Roland Young, KSAN's only African-American disc jockey, was a master of freeform radio. One night he segued from Janis Joplin live with Big Brother and the Holding Company at the Fillmore, singing "Combination of the Two," into John Coltrane's "A Love Supreme," then came out the other side with John Mayall and the Blues Breakers doing "Room to Move." While you probably had to be there, these freeform disc jockeys were true artists of musical collage.

In the early days of KSAN, I mixed rock-and-roll music into all my newscasts—maybe my old camp-mate Bob Dylan singing "Masters of War," or a line like the Jefferson Airplane's "Got a revolution, got to revolution," or the Youngbloods' "Everybody get together, try to love one another right now." I announced to the listening tribes that, "The news is the music and the music is the news." It was true. The music was our liturgy, our common anthems, the new internationales for the youth of the world.

To create a newscast, I'd take a tape recorder out into the streets and talk to people about some current issue. Then I'd mix their comments with samples of politicians making speeches, throw in lines from a few cartoon characters and some sound effects, and put it all together over a rock song or Indian raga. I often reedited politicians' speeches to make them say ludicrous things or statements that revealed the truth as I understood it. Presidents Johnson and Nixon—and later Ford and Carter as well—spoke in very regular cadences that made it fairly simple to edit or change the order and meaning of their words. Rhetoric has rhythm, even if it doesn't have soul.

Sometimes, of course, the speeches needed no editing, and I could just play a certain phrase over and over for its ironic effect. I once made a tape-loop of Richard Nixon saying, "No power on earth is stronger than the United States of America today, and none will ever be stronger than the United States of America in the future," with the added sound-effect of lightning striking. Nixon was often guilty of such classic hubris.

I kept my ukulele in the KSAN newsroom and would often pull the disc jockeys and office staff into the broadcast booth with me to do little skits or songs, like this one that summarized the news one fine day in 1969:

> *Melvin Laird has called for more Vietnamization.*
> *"We're eyeball to eyeball with the drug problem,"*
> *says the administration.*

The details of these stories, we'll leave to your imagination...(legato)...as you inhale your magic vegetation.

There were constant on-air drug references at KSAN, and listeners would occasionally hear the unmistakable sound of a DJ taking a drag of a joint. Marijuana smoking was perhaps our audience's most commonly shared behavior, a continual Delphic ritual that helped make us a tribe.

For a while, I was in charge of editing the on-air reports from Pharm Chem Labs, a commercial chemistry lab in Palo Alto that put out a weekly review of the drugs available in various neighborhoods around the Bay Area. The idea was to warn people of bad acid, badly cut heroin or cocaine, marijuana that was extra strong or had been sprayed with something toxic, and so on. The Pharm Chem people never moralized; sometimes, in fact, they sounded like the AM radio's wine connoisseurs, recommending good buys and excellent vintages.

A typical report might go something like, "In the Haight-Ashbury this week we have reports of a bunch of methamphetamine cut with baking soda. People should also be cautious about the Thai stick being sold in Berkeley in recent weeks. You may not be used to this much THC at one time..."

Pharm Chem also provided a service whereby KSAN listeners could find out exactly what it was they had bought on the street before ingesting it. For a fee, you could send in a small sample of your drugs along with a five-digit number, and then a few days later call up for a chemical analysis.

It's a truism that drugs were a central part of the 1960's counterculture, and my friends and I indulged freely. Overindulged, certainly. Just as people used to say that they only drank alcohol for medicinal purposes, I could try to claim that I only took LSD and marijuana to expand my consciousness. If my memory serves me at all, however, I mostly chose to get high for the existential kick, the sense of being present and fully alive in each moment, a feeling I would later pursue through meditation. Drug experiences also amplified my idealism, fueling images of personal and social transformation. Indeed, my friends and I saw our use of LSD and marijuana not as a problem, but as part of the solution. We could not have imagined that drugs like cocaine would become so popular, and burn up so many lives, in the years to come. At the time, we seemed to be under the protection of some good shamanic spirits.

I interviewed one San Francisco hippie who took LSD and jumped off the Golden Gate Bridge on the same day that American astronauts landed on the moon. The hippie survived his leap, and, when I visited him in his hospital room, he told me that he jumped "for spiritual advancement." He said that it didn't hurt when he hit the water because he simply left his body until the impact was over. I spliced the hippie's words together with Neil Armstrong's historic transmission, "It's one giant leap for mankind," to get a tape loop that repeated over and over: "It's one giant leap for spritual advancement." Underneath it I played the Byrds singing "Eight Miles High." LSD was our rocket to the moon. We were trying to push the limits of our earthbound imaginations.

Don't it always seem to go, but you don't know what you've got 'til it's gone. They paved paradise, put up a parking lot. O-o-o-o-w, bop bop bop bop...

JONI MITCHELL

Aside from the Vietnam War, the event that radicalized me most was the 1969 struggle over People's Park in Berkeley. In the summer of that year, it leaked out that the University of California was going to put a parking lot on a vacant square of land adjacent to the counterculture enclave of Telegraph Avenue. Hippies and radicals decided they wanted to preserve this bit of nature, so they planted a garden, set up benches, and began calling it People's Park. Although no one recognized it at the time, this was one of the early skirmishes of the environmental movement.

The battle over People's Park had all the elements of mythic theater. These young people were defying the automobile, the icon of industrial America, in order to protect a piece of nature in the heart of a city. Urban planners now acknowledge the need for "open space," and there are large environmental organizations dedicated to saving it, but back then it was simply a matter of flowers versus concrete, an instinctive reaction to the onslaught of progress. We would stop them here. We want the park and we want it—**now!**

This simple impulse led to a full-fledged battle, with troop carriers on the respectable streets of Berkeley and tear gas in the air over the prestigious campus. It got so intense that Governor Ronald Reagan finally decided to call out the National Guard. They put up a fence around the park and stationed men with rifles, bayonets at the ready, to defend it. At least a few of the Guardsmen's rifles usually had flowers sticking out of the barrels, put there by hippies to create the perfect symbol of the clashing cultures.

One day during the People's Park riots, I was hanging out on a Berkeley street corner with my tape recorder, and met three excited, long-haired radicals who were preparing for an afternoon of skirmishes with the police. They were wearing football helmets to protect their heads and gloves to protect their hands (in case the day's activities included throwing rocks or lobbing tear-gas cannisters back at the cops). As I watched, they each ceremoniously swallowed a tab of blotter acid. I was astounded. I could not imagine being stoned on LSD during a street fight. This scene may have summed up the American youth revolution of the 1960s—taking some LSD and heading off to save a piece of the planet.

While the People's Park riots were going on, I managed to get ahold of John Lennon by phone from KSAN. He was in Toronto with Yoko Ono, spending a few days "in bed for peace." Live on the air, I asked John if he had any messages for the radicals fighting for People's Park, and he replied, "Tell them all to be peaceful. We don't want any fighting going on at People's Park." The Berkeley leftists did not want to hear this message, and after the broadcast I was invited to a political consciousness-raising meeting, where people were critical of Lennon, and of me as well for not trying to convince him of the need for confrontation. But I knew that the Beatles were really a hippie band, and not so political. "All you need is love, ya da da da dah...."

I tended to agree with Lennon. Although the People's Park battles did make me more of a radical, I have never favored violence as a means of social change. I was always more of a hippie, and we believed in a kind of Gandhian nonviolence with a surrealist twist. Hippies were into street theater, not street fighting.

Just as the People's Park riots were winding down, acid guru Timothy Leary brought his own brand of theater to town, announcing that he was entering the race for governor of California against Ronald Reagan. Leary was primarily interested in exploring consciousness through LSD, but, like so many people, was drawn into the escalating political conflict between the establishment and youth culture.

Leary agreed to make his first platform statement on KSAN, and I went over to Berkeley, where he was staying, to bring him to the city. As we drove across the Bay Bridge, Leary took some LSD and offered me a tab. I could not turn down an opportunity to trip with the High Priest, and by the time we reached the KSAN studios the acid was coming on. I couldn't have delivered two coherent sentences in a row, but Leary took the microphone and calmly announced his gubernatorial candidacy:

> *Nine score and thirteen years ago, our bearded visionary forefathers brought forth on this continent, a new nation conceived in joyous revolution sparked by the Boston Tea Party, and dedicated to the proposition that we are here to be free and to turn on. I think they called it pursuit of happiness in those days. We are met here in Berkeley on a great battlefield of a civil war which now rages in this country between the turned on young, and the uptight older generation. We are going to start a new political*

*party to continue this celebration, and we are calling it the
grass roots party. I have faith that the children of the State
of California will elect me to the highest office in this
state. Let everybody come together and join the party.*

Leary's constituency may have been too stoned to get out and vote, and
Ronald Reagan was reelected. It is impossible to even hallucinate what
might have happened if Leary had won and, instead of Reagan, gone on
to become president of the United States.

While playing revolutionary on the radio, I continued to explore Asian
philosophy and mysticism. I went regularly to the San Francisco Zen
Center to hear talks by Suzuki-roshi or Alan Watts, and every Monday
night I was among the hundreds who would gather at The Family Dog, a
counterculture dance hall at Ocean Beach, where Stephen Gaskin held his
"Monday Night Class," in which he talked about LSD, Taoism, free love,
and communal living.

Karol and I also began taking tai-chi lessons. Every Saturday morning
we would walk to Chinatown, to Master Choy's class in the courtyard of
the largely Chinese YMCA. Tai-chi is a Chinese dance-yoga that brings
your consciousness down into your *tan-tien* (deep into your abdomen)
where you can find your center of gravity, as well as a sense of peace and
well-being.

After our lesson, however, we would usually walk over to Cafe
Trieste in North Beach for a sweetroll and capuccino to get the energy
moving back into our brains a little. Before long we'd invariably run into
somebody who had a joint, and, soon after, our energies would leave our
abdomens completely for the giddy highs of the mind. We didn't call ourselves "heads" for nothing.

I was also able to pursue my spiritual interests through my work at
KSAN. (During the first year that I worked there, the morning disc jockey

threw the I Ching and gave astrology reports each day.) As news and public affairs director, I would get called in to interview the Buddhist, Hindu, and Sufi teachers who were beginning to come through town more frequently in the late sixties, offering Western hippies new ways to get high. Taoism as well as Maoism found a place on the KSAN airwaves.

Many people I knew started learning meditation and yoga, joined gestalt and psychodrama groups, or began going to sweatlodges and full-moon rituals.

We plunged headlong into these experiences with a kind of foolish bravery. We were exploring the inner frontier, new states of being, new states of being, new mythologies. If our eclectic quest fell into any category, it was probably that of shamanism. We were after our own visions, outside of any church or institution, and like the traditional shamans, we often used drugs to induce them.

Even the political protests had some element of shamanism. When radicals and hippies marched on the Pentagon in 1967, they claimed to be performing an exorcism, and challenging not only our government's policy in Vietnam, but the evil spirit of materialism that had possessed a nation. The protestors surrounded the Pentagon and chanted "om" in an attempt to levitate the building. Some witnesses, to this day, claim success.

October 21, 1967, Washington, D.C., U.S.A., Planet Earth. We Freemen, of all colors of the spectrum, in the name of God, Ra, Anubis, Osiris, Tlaloc, Quetzalcoatl, Thoth, Chukwu, Olisa-Bulu-Uwa, Imales, Orisasu, Odudua, Kali, Shiva-Shakti, Great Spirit, Dionysus, Yahweh, Thor, Bacchus, Isis, Jesus Christ, Maitreya Buddha, and Rama, do exorcise and cast out the EVIL which has walled and captured the pentacle of power and perverted its use to the need of the total machine and its child the hydrogen bomb and has suffered the people of the planet, earth, the American people and creatures of the mountains, woods, streams, and oceans grievous mental and physical torture

GO OUT AND MAKE SOME OF YOUR OWN

and the constant torment of the imminent threat of utter destruction.

We are demanding that the pentacle of power once again be used to serve the interests of God manifest in the world as mankind. We are embarking on a motion which is millenial in scope. Let this day, October 21, 1967, mark the beginning of suprapolitics.

By act of reading this paper you are engaged in the Holy Ritual of Exorcism. To further participate focus your thought on the casting out of evil through the grace of GOD which is all (ours). A billion stars in a billion galaxies of space and time is the form of your power, and limitless is your name.

LEAFLET HANDED OUT AT 1967 MARCH ON THE PENTAGON

After Richard Nixon took office in 1969, the political and antiwar protests intensified. Demonstrators became more aggressive, and the government tried harder to stifle dissent. We were finally being taken seriously, often to our dismay.

One casualty at KSAN was disc jockey Roland Young, a staunch supporter of the Black Panthers. I was working in the radio station newsroom late one night. The outside buzzer rang, and when I opened the front door, I was confronted by an FBI agent, two federal attorneys, and a local cop. They were there to investigate Young for allegedly threatening the life of President Nixon on the air.

What had actually happened was that Roland had dedicated his radio show to Black Panther David Hilliard, who had been arrested that day, December 3, 1969, for a speech he had given at a huge antiwar rally in Golden Gate Park a few weeks earlier. In front of nearly 200,000 people, Hilliard had said, "We will kill Richard Nixon or anybody else who stands in the way of our freedom."

On the air, Roland had said, "For less than one dollar you could send a fifteen-word telegram to Richard Nixon saying 'I will kill Richard

Nixon or anyone else who stands in the way of our freedom.' You could do it as a gesture of support for David Hilliard. Seize the time, brothers and sisters." Roland then segued into a song called "Seize the Time," which had become the Black Panther Party's national anthem. The very next night the federal agents arrived to subpoena the tapes of Roland's show. Although the government never prosecuted him, the KSAN management immediately fired Roland. The rest of the staff protested, but eventually decided not to go on strike. We told ourselves that we needed to stay on the air to continue the struggle.

And we did just that. Until about 1974, KSAN continued to be the political underground's communication center. The Revolutionary Communist Youth Brigade, a Maoist group based in Chinatown, called me up incessantly with stories they wanted me to cover. The Weather Underground sent some of their messages to "Amerika" through KSAN, and the Symbionese Liberation Army sent most of their messages through the station, including one of the torn halves of Patty Hearst's driver's license. The SLA also sent us the famous audiotape where in Patty calls her family "the pig Hearsts" and tells them she has changed her name to Tania.

All this radical activity made life difficult for KSAN's disc jockeys, who often had marijuana around the station or on their person. We had to report communiqués immediately, or else be considered accomplices. If the federales were going to be coming over regularly to pick up the taped demands and proclamations from underground groups, then we were especially vulnerable to a drug bust.

At one point during the heyday of Symbionese Liberation Army, we set up an on-the-air code to warn each other that an SLA communiqué had arrived at the station. If you heard a disc jockey repeat "What a beautiful day, look at the blue sky" twice within a few minutes, it meant everybody should get down to the station and clean out their stashes immediately. Then and only then would some one notify the police. Our warning code worked, especially on foggy days.

Although KSAN was the voice of the radical community, we were not immune to the underground's demands for revolutionary purity. In the summer of 1971, the station held a contest to let our loyal listeners design a KSAN billboard. People sent in wonderous psychedelic drawings and paintings. Then an underground group called the Revolutionary Army bombed the Foster & Kleiser Billboard Company's headquarters in Oakland. Foster & Kleiser was owned by Metromedia, the same corporation that owned KSAN. The morning after the bombing, the Revolutionary Army sent the station a message reading, "Billboards in Babylon are an offensive manifestation of pigthink. Their fascist distortion of our people's reality can no longer be tolerated." After that, I was even more surprised that Metromedia continued to tolerate KSAN; perhaps they sensed that there was big money to made sometime down the road. I guess if revolution was profitable, it would have many corporate sponsors.

KSAN couldn't escape that basic contradiction: We were attacking the establishment while being supported by it, and worse, our rebel broadcasting was beginning to make big profits for a giant corporation. We felt like those white middle-class drop-outs, who lived on money from their parents while protesting the capitalist system. In face of the paradox, we tried our best for political purity.

For instance, the on-air staff at KSAN had constant conflicts with management and the sales department over the advertisements we were supposed to play. If a disc jockey didn't like a particular advertisement, he or she might turn the volume down so low that it was barely audible. One DJ was notorious for playing two commercials simultaneously, which, although it often made a humorous comment on consumerism, did not amuse the advertisers. Any DJ who did something like that at a radio station today would be fired immediately. Back then, KSAN's management usually just sent out a memo about how the sponsors were paying the bills, and all ads should be "showcased appropriately."

For a while, KSAN was supported mostly by advertisements from record companies and rock promoters, along with a few hip entrepreneurs trying to reach the growing counterculture population. Often, to make extra money, the air staff would help produce the commercials for these sponsors. I produced a few ads for Undulator Waterbed Company, which, believe it or not, was one of eleven different waterbed companies advertising on KSAN during the first few months of 1971. Among their competitors were: Magic Mountain Waterbeds, Waterbeds Unlimited, Neptune Waterbeds, White Tiger Waterbeds, Pasha Pillow Waterbeds, Embryo Waterbeds, Waterbed and Company, Waterbed Factory, Environmental Valve Waterbeds, and Porpoise Mouth Waterbeds. Obviously, the hippie tribes were doing their thing in comfort. To paraphrase an earlier radical, Emma Goldman, "If I can't sleep in a waterbed, I don't want to be in your revolution."

As KSAN began making real money for Metromedia, a battle began for the soul of the station. The on-air staff tried valiantly to maintain our counterculture principles and the integrity of the station's "underground" sound. When told to play a public-service announcement for the military, for example, we all refused. I remember one disc jockey trying to reason with the station manager, saying, "Hey man, you've got to remember that people are tripping out there in the audience. I don't want to be the one to bring them down with an army-recruitment ad!"

Join us in Chicago for an international festival of youth, music and theater. Rise up and abandon the creeping meatball! Come all you rebels, youth spirits, rock minstrels, truth seekers, peacock freaks, poets, barricade jumpers, dancers, lovers and artists. It is summer. It is the last week in August and the National Death Party meets to bless Johnson. We are there! There are 500,000 of us dancing in the streets, throbbing with amplifiers and harmony. We are making love in the parks. We are reading, singing, laughing, printing newspapers, groping and making a mock convention and celebrating the birth of Free America in our time.

Everything will be free. Bring blankets, tents, draft

cards, body paint, Mr. Leary's cow, food to share, music, eager skin and happiness. The threats of LBJ, Mayor Daley and J. Edgar Freako will not stop us. We are coming. We are coming from all over the world!

The life of the American spirit is being torn asunder by the forces of violence, decay and the napalm cancer fiend. We demand the Politics of Ecstasy! We are the delicate spores of the new fierceness that will change America. And we will not accept the false theater of the Death Convention. We will be in Chicago. Begin preparations now! Chicago is yours! Do it!

PRESS RELEASE, LIBERATION NEWS SERVICE, SPRING 1968

Looking back over underground newspapers from the late 1960s, I am often embarrassed by the radical left's overblown rhetoric, including some wild statements of my own. I still have a 1969 issue of *The Dock of the Bay*, a short-lived San Francisco leftist newspaper that features a picture of me as KSAN news director. Looking maniacal, I am tearing wire-copy out of a UPI teletype machine and draping it around myself, just about to take a big bite out of the news. What's embarrassing is the caption under the picture, in which I am quoted as saying, "I sometimes think that what I'm doing is incredibly revolutionary." At least that wasn't as bad as the text on the back cover of Jerry Rubin's book, *Do It! Scenarios of the Revolution*: "Jerry Rubin has written *The Communist Manifesto* of our era....comparable to Che Guevara's *Guerilla Warfare*."

Speaking of Che Guevara, in the fall of 1969 I was asked to appear with two other journalists from the alternative press on William F. Buckley's national TV show, *Firing Line*. I wore a Che Guevara T-shirt and brought along a water pistol. Buckley demolished us with his debating skills, and toward the end of the show I finally fired the squirt-gun at him. Alas, he was out of range. I must have shot myself in the foot instead.

Of course my parents were watching the show. My appearance on *Firing Line* was even announced on the front page of my hometown newspaper, the *Norfolk Daily News*. Later my mother told me that the townspeople had been very excited, stopping by my parents' shoe store on the day of the show to congratulate them in advance. The day after the show aired, however, not one citizen of Norfolk mentioned a word to my parents about having seen it.

In some ways we hippies were exactly who the conservatives thought we were: a bunch of delinquents on an extended tantrum, mad at the world for not being the paradise we had been promised by our parents and the Advertising Council of America. We didn't have goals, we had "demands." Give us kids the whole damn country, we said, and we'll show you how to run it.

Although at times during those early years at KSAN I did see myself in heroic terms, like a character from *The Sun Also Rises*, or even *War and Peace*, perhaps I was a bit closer to Don Quixote, tilting at windmills. Looking back, I sometimes think my friends and I were like kids playing capture the flag.

On the other hand, as I leaf through old radical newspapers, or listen to audiotapes from that era, I can also perceive our basic sanity. We were engaged in a serious struggle with our society, and I still think our values and understandings were, as we might have said, right on. The United States had become a militaristic imperial power, a land of excessive wealth and greed, blind to its exploitation of other peoples and its destruction of the natural world. The Woodstock generation was a thin line of resistance, as well as an early-warning system for many of the dilemmas we now face.

In the final analysis, all we ever wanted was a world of peace, justice, and joy. Is that too much to ask? We were brought up as idealists, and we simply did our best to turn our utopian visions into reality. At the very least, we did help shorten the war in Vietnam. For that reason alone there should be a statue of a hippie placed in every town square in America.

For several years Karol and I had been eager to visit Asia. Every time I interviewed a spiritual teacher, or went to hear someone speak on Zen or Hinduism, I felt the pull. Friends returned from Asia with wild tales of the great gurus and good ganja. The general idea was, "Have fun in the sun while searching for the One." The problem was that we felt too caught up in the thrills of the San Francisco counterculture and, of course, the vital work of making the revolution. Finally, one of my broadcasts set us free.

The incident involved the Chicago Eight conspiracy trial, which I had been covering from San Francisco, doing phone interviews with Abbie Hoffman, Jerry Rubin, Tom Hayden, and various members of the Black Panther party. The trial was a critical test case for the new left, because if the defendants were convicted of "conspiracy to incite riot," it would not be safe for anybody to even organize a demonstration. The antiwar movement would be paralyzed.

Always a shrewd tactician, Abbie Hoffman turned the Chicago conspiracy trial into a symbolic confrontation, calling it the trial of "the whole Woodstock generation." It was therefore appropriate, after the guilty verdict came down, that the Berkeley radicals organized a demonstration to "put the government on trial in the streets." I produced a radio spot to announce the time and place of this demonstration, and read it over the Rolling Stones singing "Street Fighting Man." I thought of being conciliatory and using the Youngbloods's "Come Together" instead, but realized that was an anthem for better times, not for the conviction of the entire Woodstock Nation.

As expected—and I'm sure it would have happened even without my announcement—the Berkeley demonstration turned into a riot of trashing and window-breaking along Telegraph and Shattuck avenues, with the usual exchange of tear gas between cops and protestors.

The next day, the *San Francisco Examiner* ran an article headlined, "Radio Tips off Protestors," accusing me of somehow provoking the riot.

I was a little flattered to think I might actually be responsible, but Metromedia's corporate lawyers were not impressed. Rather than fire me, however, and risk angering their audience, KSAN management simply told me I could no longer produce my music-and-collage newscasts. I would have to take the emotion out of my presentation. I would no longer be able to broadcast "the only news you can dance to."

I decided to quit. Listeners thought I had been fired, and protests were held outside the station, but I was secretly relieved. I was weary of my own revolutionary posturing, and I didn't like what I had become. My idealism had turned into ideology, and I was full of blame and anger. When I heard Vice President Spiro T. Agnew talk about "nattering nabobs of negativism," I, alas, recognized myself.

It was clearly time to go to Asia, and not just for a change of scene. I suspected that Eastern mysticism had something important to offer me. Maybe it could provide a cure for my cynicism, and teach me how to better love the world. Besides, I had been reading in J. Krishnamurti that a change in consciousness is "the only revolution." If so, then that revolution would have be worked on one person at a time, and maybe I should get started. Perhaps the radical transformation of society would not take place out in the streets after all, but on a meditation cushion. Idealistic American kid that I was, there was always another utopia waiting. This time it was across the ocean, on the shores of funky, cosmic India.

OUTWARD MOBILITY

Chapter Six

Such wind that scatters young
men through the world,
To seek their fortunes further
than at home
Where small experience grows.
WILLIAM SHAKESPEARE

68

One of the privileges of growing up just as America became a super-power was that many members of my generation had the leisure and the means to travel all over the world. Visiting the colonies *is* one of the perquisites of empire, and everywhere we went was our economic, if not our imperial, domain. During those mid-century migrations, America's children began absorbing symbols and stories from many, many other cultures, and bringing them back home to adorn our still-evolving millennial mythos.

Whereas the Lost Generation of American expatriots went to Europe and North Africa to feed their artistic ambitions or to experiment with socialist ideals, many of my generation went further East, seeking to evolve. Hemingway went to cover the Spanish Civil War; we charged off to do battle with the fascist powers of conditioned response and ego-domination. Orwell was down and out in London and Paris; we stayed in vermin-infested hotels in Calcutta and Katmandu on our way to ultimate liberation.

My travels were mostly to the hot lands of India and Southeast Asia, and one of the things I loved most about those places was the inevitable slowdown. In hot lands one automatically seems to move more slowly and live more simply, partly because of being a traveler passing through, of course, but also because these are places where life is lived in more intimate relation with the natural world. Most of the postindustrialized world calls it poverty. While much of it *is* just that, there is also something vital and important to be learned from those who have not yet entered the twentieth-century speed zone.

In places like Bali and India, my friends and I searched under ruins and behind Coca-Cola stands for the native secrets. We learned how to pray in the ancient temples and asked the local shamans and gurus to tell us their versions of the creation story and how they achieved salvation. We were looking for new kinds of prayer, new ways of connecting with nature and cosmos, new deities. In matters of the spirit, we were romancing the other.

> *There is nothing nobler than to put up with a few inconveniences like snakes and dust for the sake of absolute freedom.*
>
> JACK KEROUAC

Traveling through the East taught us a number of things, not least of which was a lesson in history. Strewn across the Indian landscape, for instance, are the bones of several old empires, a constant reminder of the impermanence of worldly wealth and power. The Mogul and British rulers left behind palaces and forts, many now crawling with squatters and littered with garbage. Others have been turned into museums or national historical sites tended by a surly Indian guide whose chief desire is to get your rupees and be left alone. These old ruins are testaments to the shifting fate of all nations, something you don't see much of in America.

Once when I was stuck in New Delhi waiting for a plane back to the States, I went out for a few holes of golf at the Delhi Golf Club with some friends. On one hole my ball landed on what I thought was a bunch of old bricks and rocks, and I asked my caddy if I could move it back onto the grass. "Yes, of course," he said. "These Mogul ruins are not a natural hazard." My golf ball was lying in the middle of a four-hundred-year-old archeological sand trap!

In spite of that one round of golf, and no matter what my visa said, I never really considered myself a tourist. In fact, my friends and I scorned the tourists and often made a point of avoiding the usual attractions. We were on a pilgrimage, not a vacation. We were on a quest for metaphysical sanity, not into the heart of darkness but into the light of a different kind of wisdom.

One thing I specifically wanted to find in Asia was someone who would teach me how to meditate. I was hoping for a new understanding of myself that would go beyond existential absurdity; a freedom fix deeper than politics or psychological adjustments. From childhood on, I had been a critic, habitually dissatisfied, and my judgmental mind was often as hard on me as on anything else. Conventional therapy hadn't provided much relief, and I dreamed of entering the mystic unity promised in Eastern texts and thereby losing my painful feelings of separation.

As a hippie, my spiritual search was also mixed up with the simple pursuit of pleasure. I had been seduced by the sudden, flashy insights common with LSD, and wanted no less from my meditation practice. I must have been imagining some kind of ongoing ecstacy of egolessness. Many of us were—as Tibetan Buddhist teacher Chogyam Trungpa later called us—"spiritual materialists."

And it wasn't just the cosmic highs we were after. We were intensity junkies and hard-core sensualists, and Asia promised us kicks as well as consciousness. To all chakras, to the subtle body and the gross, the East delivered.

Bali was my first stop in Asia. After quitting my job at the radio station, I flew there to meet Karol, who had gone several months earlier to study dance and music. We had decided to live in Bali for a few months, then make our way up to Nepal for a trek in the Himalayas, and finally on to India to begin our search for enlightenment. I think we were determined to get in as much fun and excitement as possible before we had to relinquish our egos to the cosmic void.

By the time I arrived in Bali, Karol was somewhat conversant in Balinese and was hanging out with a group of musicians in Ubud, an artists' village near the capital city of Denpasar. In the early '70s, Bali was still a fairly unusual travel destination, and we were treated as special guests or extremely curious creatures wherever we went.

Some evenings we would smoke some strong Sumatran marijuana and go over to the open-air shed where the Ubud gamelan orchestra was rehearsing. We were often invited to sit down right in the midst of the musicians as they played their fast, funky, syncopated Balinese gong-rock symphonies on instruments with names like kedang, reyong, kemong, trompong, cengceng, jegogan, and gedong—gedonging us right out of our minds.

The Balinese language is full of onomatopoeia, especially in musical terminology. Their bamboo xylophone is called the tingklik, because it tinkles rather than gonging like, say, the *reyongs* or other iron xylophones. Also, the Balinese names for the notes of their musical scale are ding, dong, deng, dung, and dang, and their drum-strokes are called dug and dag. This means that a Balinese tune can be started with a dag on a ding or a dang, or a dug on a deng or a dung. Dig?

Living in Bali, we began to realize how far we urban Americans had come from the way people had always lived on this planet. It was as if we were seeing backwards into a time when most of humanity worked their fields, raised their animals, and trusted both this life and the next one to the gods. My electro-techno world was epochs away from the Bronze Age scenes I witnessed on the island, and later in Nepal and India as well, where people still plowed with wooden yokes and bowed down to statues of elephant and monkey gods.

Sometimes I felt saddened by the peasants' poverty, but this feeling was usually tempered by a romantic nostalgia for what I perceived as a life of simplicity. I couldn't help but wonder if we Americans weren't suffering as much from isolation and lack of meaning in our lives as these people might be from poverty. What they had was community, as well as communion with the earth and cycles of nature—conditions which many of my urban-bred generation are consciously seeking to regain.

I fell in love with the Balinese people, admiring their sweet temperaments, and was thrilled by their art and music. I was especially delighted to hear the saying, "In Bali we do not make art. We do everything the best we can." I thought this was a truly evolved society—and then, toward the end of our stay, I heard about the so-called Communist purge of 1965.

No one knows exactly how it happened (there are rumors that the CIA was involved), but on September 30th, 1965, seven generals in the Indonesian army were killed in what the government of Prime Minister Sukarno described as an attempted Communist coup. In retaliation, the people of Indonesia began a purge of Communists and those suspected of being Communists. One of the worst bloodbaths took place on the island of Bali, where an estimated 100,000 to 300,000 Balinese were killed by their fellow citizens. Some observers say the Balinese used the purge as an excuse to resolve their ongoing feuds with one another, digging up centuries of village and family animosities. Whatever the reason, hearing about the massacre gave me pause. How could such a thing happen here in this island paradise? Again, my naive idealism was shattered.

After Bali, Karol and I flew to Nepal with several friends to do a two-week trek in the Himalayas, yet another way to get high in Asia. In 1970, Kathmandu was a hippie paradise. Not only was the city full of colorful mountain people with exotic rituals and fantastic deities, but you could also buy hashish legally in government shops! Several restaurants served cakes and pies cooked with hashish butter; one menu listed "Banana Cake Ordinaire," and just below it "Banana Cake Nirvana."

We spent six days in Kathmandu getting ready for our trek. One night after smoking several pipes full of strong Nepali hashish, I suddenly had the sense that my body was disintegrating. When I placed a hand on my chest, there was no feeling of solidity, only vague tingling sensations. I really became concerned the next morning when I woke up and still could not feel much of anything with my hands or feet. When I took hold of my toothbrush or a cup I could, again, only feel the tingling sensations and, when I took a step, it was hard for me to tell when my foot was actually touching the ground. I took some comfort in a friend's comment that it was probably the combined effects of the altitude and strong hashish, but the next day my condition worsened, and I decided to consult a Peace Corps doctor stationed in Kathmandu. He nodded knowingly as I told him my symptoms, and casually told me, "It sounds like you either have a vitamin B deficiency...or leprosy."

My friends, informed of this diagnosis, were equally casual. "Don't worry, Wes," one said. "You could stand to lose a few inches off the ears." Another told me where the local lepers' camp was located, saying "I thought you might want to stop by and see what you have to lose." I began taking megadoses of vitamin B and tried to stay calm.

The next day we boarded a small two-engine Nepali plane to fly to Pokara, where we would start our trek to the Annapurna base camp. My loss of feeling had become so severe that I could not tell if my ass was touching the plane seat or not. My body felt like a mass of tingling sensations.

I have always been a little nervous about flying, but on this occasion, I not only gave up all hope but tried to settle into the certainty of imminent death, reviewing my life and consoling myself with the thought that at least I would not have to grow old. The airplane looked like it had not been washed or serviced since World War II, and I was amazed to find graffiti scrawled on the wall right next to my seat. As soon as we took off, we began flying through steep mountain passes, flouncing wildly with the updrafts. Every time I bounced in my seat I was reminded by the tingling sensations that if I wasn't killed in the crash of this airplane, I had leprosy to look forward to.

Suddenly the plane began a steep descent. As I braced myself for a certain crash, we just as suddenly swooped upward again. When I looked out the window I saw that we had just passed over a crude airstrip bulldozed through the middle of a pasture. I later found out that the pilot routinely buzzed the strip at least once before landing, to scare the cows off the runway. When I stepped out of the airplane safely, I vowed to the gods that I would never again whine about my life. That is, until I remembered my leprosy.

For my sake, my friends delayed the start of our trek, and after several days of rest in Pokara my sense of touch began to return again. What a joy it was to feel the solidity of objects and to know that a firm earth was beneath my feet. After a few days, all of my tingling sensations had disappeared.

Three weeks later, I would encounter a great display of cosmic irony when I sat down to do my first Buddhist meditation retreat in India. The teacher gave us the following instructions: "After focusing your mind, move your attention up and down through your body, and although it may be difficult at first, try to notice all of the subtle tingling sensations that are taking place inside you. Solidity is an illusion." Although I tried hard, I could feel nothing but solidity.

After several weeks of meditation, I *was* able to feel some of the tingling again, but this time I did not experience it as a disease. I had simply become aware of the insubstantial nature of my body, on the subtlest of levels. And I began to realize that getting enlightened is somewhat like having leprosy: You have to keep giving up parts of yourself, letting them all fall away.

We have seen idols elephantine-snouted,
And thrones with living gems bestarred and pearled,
And palaces whose riches would have routed
The dreams of all the bankers in the world.

We have seen wonder-striking robes and dresses,
Women whose nails and teeth the betel stains
And jugglers whom the rearing snake caresses.
What then? What then?

CHARLES BAUDELAIRE

The hippie migration to East Asia in the late sixties was one of epic proportions. A few arrived by plane, but most came overland, in Volkswagen
vans, on local buses, hitchhiking, some even walking. Some had ditched
the Peace Corps, some were on sabbatical from perennial university
studies, others doing research on such esoteric topics as the significance of
camel dung to the early Dravidian Empire, some just on a youthful road
adventure, others trying to find or lose themselves or discover something
missing from their lives. Many were simply seeking thrills, usually in the
form of cheap and plentiful Asian drugs. Quite a few of us were on our
way to do the full-circle spiritual tour, from the Himalayan caves to the
South Indian Theosophical Society. We were looking for cosmic truths, a
guru (mother, father) we could call our own, or a spiritual path that fit
the curve of our souls.

Most Westerners traveled to the East on a route that the hippies soon
dubbed the "hashish road." This series of bumpy highways started anywhere in Europe and wound across Turkey, where many were long de-
tained for some hassle or another, and then through the deserts of Iran
and Afghanistan, still easily passable in the late '60s and early '70s,
where travelers often lingered for some hashish-dream days wandering
the narrow streets of Kabul in search of a trippy looking mosque. The
hippies' eyes were as wide with wonder as Marco Polo's must have been,
but usually with dilated pupils.

The hashish road soon became littered with strung-out, destitute young people, some sick with amoebic dystentery or hepatitus, many half insane from culture shock, their illness and disorientation amplified by Afghani and Kashmiri hashish, Thai stick, psilocybin mushrooms, or the high-grade Pakistani and Chinese opium and heroin.

Eventually, some concerned Westerners organized ways to help this traveling Haight-Ashbury of the East. In Kathmandu, for instance, a few people created an informal travelers' aid center in a restaurant called the Bakery. If you were lost, broke, addicted, or just wanted information about a good ashram, the people at the Bakery could help. They offered yoga and meditation classes, free food and warm clothing, and sometimes even money to get back to the West.

A multitude of bizarre and amazing tales arose from the hippie migration to the East. A notable one is of Michael Riggs, a San Diego surfer who headed off to Europe in 1966 and eventually found himself hanging out in Greece with a Russian princess named Zena. They traveled to India, where Zena went her own way after deciding that she was the reincarnation of the nineteenth-century spiritualist Madame Blavatsky. Michael Riggs, meanwhile, became an Indian sadhu through and through. He put a single cloth, a *longi*, around his body, matted his long curly hair with ashes, and began wandering barefoot around India from holy place to holy place, singing Hindu devotional songs and playing an *ektar*, a one-stringed instrument. Michael Riggs, the surfer from San Diego, was eventually given the name Bagawan Das by his guru, Neem Karoli Baba, and later became famous for leading psychologist Richard Alpert to this very same teacher. Soon thereafter, Richard Alpert became Baba Ram Dass and went back to America to write *Be Here Now*, the book that launched another, even bigger wave of Western seekers onto the shores of cosmic India.

It was a lark for us to live on the cheap; a kind of contest to see who could stay in Asia the longest time on the least money. The competition was tough. I knew people who came to India or Nepal with just a few hundred dollars and stayed for years. They begged and scrounged, they sold their passports or pulled some lost-travelers-check scam, they went from ashram to ashram and temple to temple, living off the *prasad* (holy offerings). One couple who did Buddhist meditation retreats with me made money to stay on in India by smuggling Buddha statues filled with hashish back to the West.

Another traveler's triumph was to go where no one else had gone before, or to be present at some esoteric ritual that few white people had ever seen. One hippie I knew learned Hindi and adopted the life of the wandering holy man completely, but was still refused entry into a special Hindu temple that was restricted to the upper castes. Being a foreigner meant he was casteless, but this hipster was determined to get inside that temple anyway. Finally, after fasting for four days on the temple steps he succeeded. After that, his reputation on the travelers' circuit was made.

Those of us who stayed in the East for any length of time began to adopt the local styles of dress. We stopped wearing shirts and pants, replacing them with various pieces of cloth. In India and Southeast Asia, the traditional clothing does not have buttons or zippers, snaps or belts. When you get up in the morning you don't get dressed, you get wrapped.

I eventually accumulated many different pieces of fabric of all shapes and sizes: dhotis, longis, sarongs, shawls, scarves, and so on. Each piece has a specific function, but often I would see Westerners wearing something around their head that was meant for their waist, or vice versa. It's all just cloth, anyway. Wind it around your neck, midriff, and loins, and you were wrapped up for the day!

Despite our fascination with the culture, India inevitably wore us down. The bad food made us weak and susceptible to various illnesses, and we'd grow weary of the crowds and intensity. Then it was time to call on our privileged birth and head for the white man's refuges—the imperialist enclaves of a first-class British or American hotel. We usually couldn't afford to rent rooms, but we often spent a day just roaming around the lobbies, acting as though we had a reservation.

The British hotels are the most elegant, appointed with the formerly subjugated people's finest carpets, furniture, vases, and artwork. In India these havens for the Raj rulers are always set back from the streets, with doormen and handlers waiting to serve you and to keep out the street vendors and riffraff. The British stayed in these hotels on their travels and business trips through their colonies, insulated from the jungle and the strange native ways.

Sometimes we went to the American hotels—the Sheratons, the Hiltons, and the Sheraton Hiltons—in whose lobbies and lounges we would find the looser and glitzier style of the new American corporate world and the international jet set. You could usually buy jeans, the latest music, and even a hamburger or pizza in these lobbies. At least you could buy something that *looked* like a hamburger or pizza. The new imperialists were bringing the questionable wonders of American culture to the world.

Sometimes we would grab a little nap on one of the soft lobby chairs, or sit in the air-conditioned cafe for hours, reading and talking. And then, after a decent supper at the hotel coffeeshop, we would fade away to our own roach-infested hotels on the other side of town where the poor Arabs lived, or over by the train station where we were guaranteed a night of strange noises in bare rooms teeming with terrible tropical bugs and vicious viruses.

The worst part of our expatriot days was the inevitable illnesses. The subcontinent's bugs seemed to love the fat blood of Westerners, and almost everyone who spent more than a few months in India or Nepal came down with some strange disease.

Once in Dharmsala, India, after feeling slightly feverish and listless for a few days, I visited the local Tibetan medical clinic. The complete and official name of this establishment was The Tibetan Medical and Astro Institute which should have given me a clue as to the type of medicine they practiced.

I explained my symptoms to a sweet Tibetan lady, who breastfed her baby while diagnosing my condition. She then handed me several sheets of paper describing various Tibetan pills that I might want to try. One was the "Chakril Chenmo" or Great Iron Pill, touted as a blood purifier and excellent for sluggishness and fevers, as well as all eye ailments. This wonder pill consists of forty different ingredients, including "purified iron filings, three myrobalans without seeds, Kashmiri saffron, musk, solidified bile of elephant, saxifrage pasumensis marg, purified magnetic stone, addatoda vasica, sea shells, white and red sandal woods, meconopsis species, costus roots, Indian valerian, rhino horn, and asphaltum." The solidified bile of elephant didn't bother me as much as "asphaltum" which I guessed was ground up pieces of highway. Most such Tibetan pills come with the instructions: "If possible one should recite the mantra of the medicine Buddha 'Tadyatha aum bhaishjya maha bhaihjya raja samud gate svaha' and the mantra of Avalokitesvara 'Aum mani padme hum' as many times as possible before taking the pill."

What finally cured me of my ailment, I believe, was lots of Nepali chicken soup. Joseph Campbell may have found common myths throughout the world, but in my travels I made an equally important discovery: the universal sanctity of chicken soup. From an early age I was fed chicken soup as the Jewish cure for all kinds of *tzuris*, from flu to depression, but I never suspected that, in fact, chicken soup is a panacea of mythic proportions throughout the world.

Everywhere I have gone on the planet, people were cooking up chicken soups. With regional ingredients added—sambal and rice in Indonesia, cilantro and noodles in Nepal, curry and rice in India, lime, chiles, and potatoes in Mexico and Guatemala, wontons, noodles, and chiles in China and Thailand, matzoh balls, celery, and carrots in New York—chicken soups offer the requisite nutrients for psychic as well as physical healing.

I even have a theory—discussed with a few paleontologists and anthropologists without coming to any firm conclusion—that chickens are so dear to us because they were our first food after we left the trees for the tall grasses. In those grasses we happened to find these tasty birds who couldn't fly.

Many of us who have taken on the Buddhist ethic, with its regard for all sentient beings, try to justify the continued consumption of chicken soups. I myself rationalize that chickens are barely sentient. They are more nearly like a vegetable than a bird; a walking vegetable with such a limited range of movement that it always stays close to the cookpot.

Only mad dogs and Englishmen go out in the noonday sun.

RUDYARD KIPLING

Most travelers to the East had a regular circuit that they followed, usually dictated by the seasons. Many of us spent our winters in the plains of India, visiting gurus and studying in ashrams. By March, when it started getting really hot, it was time to begin making your way up toward the Himalayas, either to Nepal or to the Indian hill stations, where you could spend the summer hanging out with the sweet mountain people, trekking or maybe studying in a Tibetan Buddhist monastery. In the fall we would head back down to the plains again, and finally, to the yearly Christmas bash on the golden beaches of Goa, where many hundreds of Western travelers would gather to dance, take drugs, and exchange mystical practices and tales of their Asian adventures.

Another part of the travelers' circuit led through Southeast Asia. Indian visas lasted for only three months and, unless you could find a good excuse to get an extension, you would have to leave India for a while before being allowed to return. While some people would conveniently lose their passports or simply risk getting caught with an outdated visa in order to remain in India, many travelers headed farther East for a few months.

A common odyssey was to fly or boat to Thailand, journey by train down through Malaysia to Singapore, take a boat across the South China Sea to Jakarta and a train across Java to Bali, and then reverse directions and make your way back up to India. These trips through the soft, sweet lands of Southeast Asia were a chance to recuperate from the diet and diseases of India and Nepal. One could spend time on the beaches of Thailand and Malaysia and Indonesia, swimming in the warm ocean to wash off accumulated grime, eating seafood and fruit to gain strength for yet another stint chasing enlightenment on the subcontinent.

When we gathered at the travelers' hotels in Singapore or Bangkok, we would trade stories of our adventures. I used to tell about the time I rode all night through the jungles of Sumatra on a bus jammed with peasants and their animals. What made this trip peculiar was that the bus driver drove along singing pop songs into a microphone that had been hooked up over his seat. The singing driver was accompanied by a man who sat next to him and played a small electric organ that was propped up on the dashboard. Most astonishing, however, was the fact that a big loud-speaker was mounted on top of the bus, so that as we rode along through the night this live performance went booming out over the jungle. I never could find out if there was a reason for this—maybe it was to warn on-coming traffic or scare away thieves but—I imagined prowling tigers and big-eyed owls astounded by this rambling Sumatran jukebox-bus and the driver's heavily accented "r-r-r-ollin', r-r-r-olin' onna rivah...."

We really had gone to Asia to find a meditation teacher or guru and so, after our trek in Nepal, Karol and I took a wild bus ride down the mountains into India to begin our search. Our first stop was Varanasi, the holiest city in a nation full of holy cities, the birthplace of Lord Shiva, the deity who rules over life and death.

Varanasi marks the spot where, three thousand years ago, a group of sages sat down on the banks of the Ganges River and began to intuit the size of the cosmos and explain the karma of the universe. The mystics who wrote the Upanishads lived in Varanasi, and later the Buddha himself came here to "turn the wheel of the law" and begin his teachings in a nearby forest.

It was thus appropriate, in many ways, that I was given my first lesson in Eastern spiritual practices in Varanasi, on those auspicious banks of the Ganges—by a hashish-smoking Shiva baba. Considered to be one of the world's oldest religious cults, the Shiva babas number in the millions in India. They are wanderers, moving from holy place to holy place, continuously praying to Lord Shiva, and sometimes using hashish to get in touch with him. Of course, we hippies were very attracted to these homeless, dope-smoking mystics.

One of my first days in Varanasi, I was sitting down by the cremation grounds watching the bodies go up in smoke when this crazy-looking old man with matted hair, naked except for a loincloth, his face streaked with ash marks and painted with red designs, ambled up to me and said, "Hello, my friend, what do you want?" At first I thought he wanted to sell me something, so I shook my head and turned away. But then he said, "Are you looking for something here in India?" I turned and appraised him, and finally decided to answer. "Liberation. Freedom. That is what I am seeking in India."

"Then follow me," he said. And without a look back he turned and walked down toward the river.

After a few minutes I got up and followed him, and by the time I had reached the spot where he was sitting he had already laid out a piece of cloth on the sand, placed a chillum pipe on it, and was busy rubbing a piece of hashish with tobacco to prepare us a smoke.

After I smoked a pipe with this holy fool, I asked him if he could give me any advice on how to become enlightened. As soon as he began to speak, I realized that he didn't care whether I became his disciple or not, that he wanted nothing from me but my company over a bowl or two of hashish.

"I will give you one important piece of advice," he said. "No matter what prayers or meditations you are doing, be sure to awaken before the sun comes up. Then you will have a chance to calm and focus your mind after sleeping, before the light of the sun comes to reveal all the world to you and distract you from yourself." I bow down to my Shiva baba for that advice. May he have many a nice day.

While Varanasi is the holiest city in India, it is also the center of the Indian silk trade, and thousands of touts and hustlers will assault you from the minute you arrive until the minute you leave, beseeching you, "Come, see best silk, give good price. My family store, only look, come now, special price." In Varanasi, the silk trade is second only to the business with the gods.

One morning, when I had nothing else to do, I went into a nicely appointed silk store a bit early, just as the proprietor was arranging his stock for the day's commerce. A handsome middle-aged Indian man in Western pants and blazer, he greeted me in fluent English. With his dark brown eyes, black hair, and mildly hooked nose he could have passed for a middle-class Jewish businessman in New York or Chicago. In fact, he somewhat resembled my father, right down to his fine manners. I was comforted by the scene's familiarity, until I turned around and saw this respectable businessman light a stick of incense and begin praying to a statue of the elephant god Ganesha which was perched on an altar next to his cash register. It was one thing to see the wild-looking street people praying to elephant and monkey gods, but to see this prosperous, and presumably well-educated gentleman bowing down before his idol was somehow incongrous and shocking to me. On my next visit to my parents, I told my father this story and showed him a picture of Ganesha. He laughed and laughed. "Imagine," my father said, "praying to an elephant!" I wanted to ask my father what his god looked like, but my tongue cleaved to the roof of my mouth. I also didn't tell him that I was a little jealous of Hinduism's colorful deities and images. The one and only God I grew up with would not let Himself be seen, and maybe that's why I had such a hard time finding Him.

All India is full of holy men stammering gospels in strange tongues; shaken and consumed in the fires of their own zeal; dreamers, babblers, and visionaries: as it has been from the beginning and will continue to the end.

RUDYARD KIPLING

India was full of gods and gurus. The biggest problem was that there were so many to choose from. Some Westerners came to India to stay at a specific Hindu ashram, like those founded by one of the famous old masters such as Yogananda or Ramakrishna, or one run by a hot-shot lineage-holder whose fame had spread to the West, like the Beatles' guru, Maharishi Mahesh Yogi, or Ram Dass's guru, Neem Karoli Baba. Others became disciples of more obscure Indian yogis. I met one young woman from Ohio who found her guru living in a tiny wooden box in Varanasi. People in the neighborhood said that this holy man had not spoken in thirty years, so this fresh-faced young midwestern girl just sat outside the box every day for nearly a year, content to be near him and "feel his presence." A young man I knew from upstate New York moved into a Himalayan cave in order to be near his wild mountain guru. He stayed for almost six months, until one night both of them were chased away by a tiger.

Like many others, Karol and I did a little guru-hopping ourselves, checking out the various spiritual scenes. I had interviewed a yogi named Swami Satchitananda on the radio back in San Francisco in 1969, and he had told me that I looked just like Satya Sai Baba, especially my wild kinky hair, and said that if I ever got to India I must go visit this holy man. Satya Sai Baba was considered an incarnated deity by millions of people in southern India, and was said to be able to materialize objects out of thin air. His disciples dug him so much they called him *Sri Sri Sri* Satya Sai Baba. We tried to track him down at his various ashrams, but kept missing him. As a consolation, his disciples smeared our foreheads with magical ashes he apparently had materialized.

We did find Bhagwan Sri Rajneesh at his ashram, however, and since this was before his rise to fame, we easily gained an audience with him. Rajneesh had us try one of his "chaotic meditations," encouraging us to twirl around and around as fast as possible, all the while shouting "Who? Who? Who?" After a full half-hour of this dizzying hyperventilation and self-questioning we were told to fall to the floor and lie there quietly listening for the answer. All I ever got was silence and a little nausea, which may indeed be the answer.

Rajneesh's way of teaching Westerners was a lot like a Hindu version of gestalt therapy. Eventually he told his disciples to act out all their wildest desires for sensual pleasures before trying to find inner peace. In the end we all learned an important lesson from Rajneesh: that indulging yourself with one Rolls Royce doesn't necessarily mean that you won't decide to indulge yourself with another Rolls Royce. At last count, I heard he ended up with seventy-five of them.

Swami Muktananda was another one of the heavies, the Hindu equivalent of a hip Catholic cardinal in a big American diocese, a guru with real power and lineage behind him. Muktananda was a spiritual guide to some of Bombay's wealthiest Indians, counting among his admirers none other than Indira Gandhi. We were fortunate enough to drive up to his ashram near Bombay just after sunset, so we got a good view of the huge neon "Om" sign that was visible for several miles around.

Despite the cabaret-like sign, inside Muktananda's ashram we found an unmistakable vibration, a tangible atmosphere of peace and purity common to many of India's monasteries and holy places. Sai Baba's ashram and Neem Karoli Baba's temples had the same quality, possibly the effect of years of incessant prayer and meditation. Just walking into one of these sanctuaries was like entering another world. This was partially due, no doubt, to the contrast between their cleanliness and calm and the chaos of India just outside.

As we traveled around the spiritual circuit, we kept hearing about this or that teacher who had a shortcut to enlightenment or who specialized in teaching Westerners or had miraculous powers. It seemed that on every

Himalayan peak and in every ashram on the Deccan plain another guru was offering a better bliss and an emptier emptyness. Meanwhile, many young Westerners, always on the lookout for the ultimate exotic experience, became fascinated by tales of certain yogis who practiced the mysterious tantric arts.

Tantra is an esoteric school of yoga and meditation that attempts to harness all human energies in the service of higher consciousness. Through the ages, tantric masters have devised all sorts of rituals to stir up our deepest subconscious fears and desires, and then to work with and transform them. For example, students of tantra are often instructed to meditate all night among the corpses at cremation grounds, contemplating their own death.

Since sex is one of the most powerful human drives, the tantric masters try to work with this energy through specially designed techniques. In tantric sex one prolongs intercourse by deepening the breath and coordinating it with one's partner, blending the male and female energies until there is no longer any separation. After an extended period of practice, the couple ostensibly arrives at the unified state of consciousness that existed before the separation of male and female, or yin and yang—which is to say, before creation itself.

There is no climax in the tantric sexual union; no orgasm or ejaculation. Instead, all energy generated in the genital region gets channeled to the higher centers, or chakras. The way I once heard it described was that male tantric adepts would reverse their ejaculate and drive it up their spines, to literally blow their minds.

Westerners loved stories about the tantric masters. I remember listening to some people who had come down from a remote Tibetan ashram in Sikkim with tales of yogis who had so much control over their genital muscles that they could suck milk up into their body through their penises. Their female consorts were said to be able to play the trumpet with their vaginas. Some hippies thought these were fun-sounding things to do, not realizing that such powers are the product of years of rigorous training and renunciation. Many of us were drawn to tantra by the possiblity of prolonged sexual pleasure, but we eventually—maybe a little grudgingly—came to understand that tantra is about the end of personal pleasure. In fact, it's about the end of personal anything.

My first real initiation into Eastern wisdom, which is to say my first meditation retreat, took place in Bodhgaya, India, in the winter of 1970 (the time when I tried to get back my tingling sensations). Karol and I had heard about an excellent Buddhist meditation teacher from Burma, S.N. Goenka, who was traveling around India offering ten-day meditation retreats. He taught a very basic Buddhist practice called *vipassana*, or insight meditation, which was said to be an accessible, no-frills path to inner peace and freedom. People dubbed Goenka "the singing guru" because of the deep, beautiful baritone in which he chanted the Buddhist sutras every morning and evening during his retreats.

Goenka had once been a wealthy Indian businessman in Rangoon. His family and his business collegues say he was something of a tyrant and prone to fits of anger. He was also tortured by migraine headaches, and traveled to the best medical clinics in London and Switzerland, searching in vain for a cure. Finally, Goenka met a Buddhist teacher who lived just a few blocks from his house in Rangoon, and soon found that insight meditation helped bring an end to both his headaches and his temper. He was so grateful that he decided to devote his life to teaching others.

Although we originally signed up to meditate for only ten days with Goenka, we ended up staying a month, doing three retreats one after the other. After each night's final meditation session we would gather in the hall or in somebody's hut and talk, sometimes until sunrise, about what we were learning and how it related to Western psychology and philosophy, or to our lives back home. We were practicing a meditation technique that involved moving the mind up and down the body, from head to toe and back again in a rhythmic and repetitive manner, focusing on bodily sensations. Goenka called this process "sweeping." I asked Goenka if we were eventually going to "sweep ourselves out of existence." We were all very excited by the notion of getting rid of our egos.

Those who came to sit with the singing guru in Bodhgaya included Ram Dass and a few of his entourage, Joseph Goldstein and Sharon Salzberg, who later became meditation teachers and cofounders of one the largest Buddhist centers in the United States, Daniel Goleman, who became the *New York Time's* behavioral sciences editor, a woman named Tsultrim Allione who wrote a seminal book on women's spirituality, and many others who eventually became teachers and translators, smuggling the true treasures of the East back home with them.

During one course, at the full moon, Goenka took us to the Mahabodhi Temple in Bodhgaya, to sit in meditation under the very tree where the Buddha was enlightened. It was all so romantic and exotic, and I remember thinking that we were pioneers of consciousness, discovering a secret truth that would transform us and maybe even change the world.

After the Bodhgaya meditation retreats were over, Ram Dass hired a bus to take people to visit his Hindu teacher, Neem Karoli Maharaji. Karol and I were invited to go along, but instead embarked on our futile search for Satya Sai Baba.

That busload of our friends hung out with Neem Karoli Maharaji for a while, and eventually, almost all of them received new spiritual names from the guru. Linda Thurston became Mirabai, Sandy Miller became Tara, Danny Goleman became Jaggernath Dass, Jeffery Miller became Surya Dass, Jim Litton became Rameshwar Dass, and so on. The suffix "dass" in Hindi means "servant of," so Ram Dass is literally "the servant of Ram."

I must say I was rather jealous of the people who were on that bus. They not only got to be with Ram Dass's famous guru but they received new names to boot. Later my wife Karol got a new name from our teacher Goenka. She became Mudita, which in the Pali language means "selfless joy." Eventually, I just decided to make up my own spiritual name. I started calling myself "What's Up Dass," or, "the servant of what's up." It's a perfect name for a journalist.

Perhaps the fact that I missed both Satya Sai Baba and Neem Karoli Maharaji was the universe's way of keeping me on the Buddha's path. During my time in India I learned a lot from Hindu teachers, and I was enchanted by the Hindu pantheon of dieties, which, in their archetypal displays, remind me somewhat of the Greek gods and goddesses. However, I never felt completely comfortable in the Hindu yogic system. Besides, all of my early influences, from the beatniks on, had been pointing me toward the teachings of the Buddha, and that was the path I started walking in India.

INWARD MOBILITY

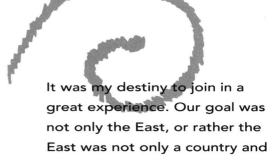

It was my destiny to join in a great experience. Our goal was not only the East, or rather the East was not only a country and something geographical, but it was the home and youth of the soul, it was everywhere and nowhere, it was the union of all times.

HERMAN HESSE, *A JOURNEY TO THE EAST*

So why would a nice Jewish boy from Nebraska travel to the other side of the planet to study Buddhist meditation, embracing a practice that involves sitting on the floor rather than in a nice chair? The Jewish people let their forelocks grow as a sign of piety, the Buddhists shave their heads. The Jews wail and beat their breasts in front of their God, the Buddhists sit silently in cool detachment.

Of course, it is impossible to know for sure why anyone gets caught in a particular endgame of psycho-spiritual liberation, or search for enlightenment, as it is better known. Some sages say that a spiritual calling is the result of past lives and accumulated good karma. Scientists might discover it has something to do with genetics—maybe people attracted to mystical pursuits will turn out to have a double helix twisted into a yin-yang symbol. All I know for certain is that there were definite cultural forces pulling me around to the other side of the planet and back through the centuries into the lap of the Buddha.

Historian Arnold Toynbee said that the transmission of Eastern spiritual practices to the West would turn out to be the most significant event of the twentieth century, and my generation was the first to embrace those practices in any significant number. At mid-century there were only a handful of Hindu or Buddhist centers outside of Asia. Today, hundreds of thousands of people in America, Europe, and Australia are twisting their unwilling legs into awkward variations on the classic lotus position. Catholic girls from Chicago, instead of moving down the rosary beads reciting, "Hail Mary, full of grace," are moving beads around their Tibetan *malas* and chanting, "Om Mane Padme Hum," while Jewish boys from Long Island have taken on improbable Hindu and Buddhist names and are chanting "Hare Krishna," "Jai Ram," or "Om Shanti," phrases that will no doubt replace "Shema Yisroel" on their lips at the moment of death. Hospitals throughout the West now use ancient Eastern meditation techniques for stress and pain reduction, and major universities are studying yogis and meditators to see if "consciousness" can be improved upon, or indeed, actually engaged for the first time. Eastern wisdom seems to have settled in the West for a while. Perhaps it has come to help us sooth our jangled nerves or dissolve our overblown egos before it's too late.

Of course, some Westerners had discovered Buddhist dharma or Hindu Vedanta long before my generation. British intellectuals who were stationed in or visiting their country's imperial outposts became fascinated with Chinese and Indian religious traditions. Most of these Brits, however (with a few notable exceptions), saw Eastern spiritual practices as little more than curiosities to be written up in travel books or anthropological papers. Remember that the British controlled the Far East's spice trade for centuries without ever learning how to use those spices in their own cooking. When it came to Eastern wisdom, the British never learned how to, as the yogis say, "cook themselves."

Perhaps it was simply a matter of timing. (Much the same thing happened on the North American continent, as Europeans disregarded the wisdom of the indigenous tribes they conquered.) Not until the turn of the century and the emergence of modern psychology did the great teachings of Taoism, Buddhism, and Hinduism start to gain broader acceptance in the West. The psychologists were the shock troops who first blasted through the concrete shell that is the autonomous, rational, Western self.

Until Freud and his followers came along, most Westerners had unwavering faith in the rational mind, believing it to be in firm control of the person it inhabited. However, as Eric Fromm pointed out in his 1960 study *Zen Buddhism and Psychoanalysis*, "Freud did not share the high evaluation of our conscious thought system, so characteristic of Western man." Freud's great contribution was to show us that we are not as highly evolved as we think. And given that he studied members of the European middle and upper classes, perhaps it should come as no great surprise that Freud would come to view the entire species as somewhat disturbed.

> *May we not be justified in reaching the diagnosis that, under the influence of cultural urges, some civilizations or some epochs of civilization— possibly the whole of mankind—have become "neurotic."*
>
> SIGMUND FREUD

Western psychology raised questions that led many of my generation to doubt our understanding of ourselves. Since our religions supplied no satisfying answers, some of us turned to the ancient Hindu and Buddhist techniques of self-investigation. In meditation practice—that is to say, in ourselves—we found a more humbling and realistic view of the human condition.

In addition, we were starved for a new system of cosmology and mythology, especially one that better fit our modern scientific understanding. In our lifetime, astronomers had found great clusters of galaxies, each full of billions of stars, and the old earth-centered Judeo-Christian universe just couldn't accomodate such an expanse. In contrast, the Eastern sages had long ago painted a vast picture of time and space. In one Buddhist text, the universe is called three-thousand-fold, because it contains one thousand times one thousand times one thousand world systems similar to our own. Meanwhile, the Hindu conception of time stretches out far beyond the big bang. The Hindu creator diety, Brahma, lives for 31,000 billion years, and when one Brahma dies, another Brahma is born. Along with him is born another universe. According to the Hindu text, the *Brahmavaivarta Purana*, "Brahma follows Brahma; one sinks, the next arises; the endless series cannot be told."

Modern science prepared us for Eastern mysticism. In the 1940s and 1950s, the worldview prevalent in quantum physics was just beginning to trickle down into the collective psyche. The generation born mid-century was the first to read about relativity in their schoolbooks, giving us the notion that reality was a subjective experience. We were the first generation to be taught that space and time are actually the inseparable "space-time," and matter and energy the inseparable "matter-energy." In college we might have started hearing about quantum paradoxes, wave/particle dualities, and nonlinear realities. These ideas implied that everything in our universe was tightly woven together in a nonlogical, nonmechanical way, quite different than what our senses perceived or our civilization had always believed. And so, when we finally began to hear about the Buddhist and Hindu worldviews, there was a deep resonance.

Of course, I attribute several degrees of my own turn Eastward to my association with the beatniks, who were infatuated with Zen, and several more degrees to the hippies and their love affair with both Hinduism and Buddhism. Another seminal experience for me, and for many others who may be cautious about admitting it these days, was LSD—the sacrament of the sixties.

Acid helped many people temporarily remove the fictions of ego and separation that seem to engulf much of humanity. At its most benevolent, LSD could offer a direct experience of interdependence with all things, and, furthermore, help open one's heart to the world. It turns out that Taoists, Hindus, and Buddhists were already quite well-versed in these feelings of oceanic oneness and compassion, and we found that our visionary drug experiences were often best explained by Eastern spiritual texts. Timothy Leary and his colleagues advised using *The Tibetan Book of the Dead* and the *Tao Te Ching* for guidance during LSD sessions. Many people came to understand that what they were experiencing on LSD was not just hallucinatory play, but a traditional mystical perception of reality. Later, after the drug's psychological hazards became apparent, and the adage "you never have to come down" proved false, some of us began to try the more practical, if much more difficult, Eastern ways into the mystic. We realized we had to start from the bottom up rather than the top down.

Maybe, in the end, I was attracted to Buddhist meditation because of the smile on the Buddha's face. "No smiling" seems to be an unwritten commandment of most religions. The major texts rarely display any humor, or even bemusement at the human predicament. There are no jokes or cartoons in the Bible or the Koran, and we can only infer that the God who dictated these books had no sense of humor. Nowhere does it say that Abraham or Jesus or Muhammad ever laughed, and it seems that none of them, heaven forbid, ever told a joke.

There are no jokes in the Buddhist Pali Cannon either, but at least the Buddha smiles. He seems to be the only religious figures who does, unless you count tricksters like Coyote, who are usually laughing because they've just turned the world upside down and made it harder for humans to find their way.

The Buddha smiles because he's got a way out for everybody. From his lotus seat he watches the drama and says, "This too shall pass." Even better, he designed some great exercises that will bring a smile to anyone's face, even in the midst of life's inevitable suffering. Of course, the smile is just the hook. Once you're caught, the hard work begins.

To study Buddhism is to study the self. To study the self is to know the self. To know the self is to forget the self.

ZEN MASTER DOGEN

The first task in most schools of meditation is to deconstruct the self. It's the last deconstruction you'll ever need to do, because after you deconstruct the deconstructor, the world becomes whole again.

During my first meditation retreats in India in 1970, I was shocked to discover that I was not who I thought I was. Furthermore, I was not my thoughts. I was not my thinking mind.

This revelation came as I was trying to stay focused on my breathing, as I'd been instructed—inbreath...outbreath...inbreath...outbreath—and somehow my mind, against my will, continued to think. As I meditated, I slowly began to realize that my mind has a mind of its own.

This was devastating. We tend to believe that we can control our thoughts, that they are real, and that they are, in essence, us. Meditation allowed me to step out of my thinking mind and witness its mechanisms and machinations. Instead of paying a shrink good money to listen to my psychic babble and nod his head every ten minutes, I found I could do it myself for free. The technique I learned in India, insight meditation, is a way of sneaking behind the self, disengaging awareness from the contents of one's psyche so as to become a silent observer. Establishing this internal "other" may be the closest we can get to objectivity about ourselves.

And what did I find when I began to investigate myself in meditation? As the ancient saying goes, self-knowledge is usually bad news. I saw that I was ruled by a confusion of neurotic voices, full of desire and envy and self-absorption. Not until later did I find that buried under all of this was a completely different person, full of clarity and compassion and

Inward Mobility

contentment; someone I could live with and would spend the rest of my life trying to uncover.

I found that my journalistic skills came in handy for meditation practice. Reporters, like meditators, are trained to be objective, dispassionate observers of events, and both believe that only truth can liberate us. The main difference is that in meditation the story being covered is oneself.

On one of my first meditation retreats in India, the journalist inside me joined forces with my meditative witness to record what it sounds like inside my mind. Here's a few moments of it. Take my mind. Please.

> *Ahhhh, inbreath...outbreath...I'm resolved to stay focused on my breath this hour...inbreath...I'll just move my knee over a little...there...oh no...that position's going to make my knee sore before too long...I'll just move it back...I hope nobody was looking...I should be sitting perfectly still in this practice...okay, now just stay with this position...outbreath...maybe I should count my breaths for a while until my mind gets settled...inbreath one...outbreath...inbreath two...outbreath...if I can get up to twenty-five I'll start over...inbreath three...whoa, did I miss one breath?...I can't remember...okay, I'll start over with inbreath one again...darn...darn?...did I just judge myself for losing count? I'm not supposed to judge myself in this practice...outbreath...now I'm judging myself for judging myself...oh no...what a mess these synapses are...luckily it's not really me...Okay, so concentrate!... Inbreath one...outbreath...inbreath two...now we're getting down to it...outbreath...Let me take you down, 'cause I'm going to, Strawberry Fields...what a great song that is...I wonder whatever happened to Laura...the days we spent in Golden Gate Park together...what a wonderful time we had!...am I less optimistic now?...optimistic, optical mistake...optimal mystic...that's a cute wordplay...*

write that down later... whoa...okay, time to meditate... inbreath one...outbreath...inbreath two...or is that three? ...why is this so hard? Is anyone else having such a difficult time. Better look around. Whoops, I'm supposed to keep my eyes closed in this practice...living is easy with eyes closed...I'll bet the Beatles weren't practicing this damn meditation technique...and why am I always humming something...my mind has been destroyed by rock and roll...okay, back to the task...inbreath one...outbreath ...inbreath two...outbreath...now we're getting the rhythm ...inbreath three...if I meditate real good this hour then I'll go for a walk and relax...outbreath...or I'll go sit in the dining room and watch the other yogis...I wonder if that cute girl with the purple zafu is lovers with the guy she came to registration with...what great eyes...oh no, here come the dirty movies...forget it, she won't make me happy...this is just lust...lust...lusting...LUSTED...Hey, it went away...the objective witness of mindfulness strikes again!..okay, back to the breath...get serious...inbreath one...I could die in the next minute...outbreath...inbreath two...outbreath...inbreath three...outbreath...Alright! I can feel my mind getting more spacious...inbreath four...outbreath...inbreath five...nice, nice...I like this feeling...outbreath...a little concentration brings a little peace of mind...inbreath six...I should sit more often...outbreath ...Nothing is real, nothing to get hung about, Strawberry Fields forever....

After weeks of watching this kind of internal dialogue spin itself out, I began to take *all* of my thoughts less seriously. Instead of identifying almost excusively with my thinking mind, I started to experience the center of my being in my breath. In the final analysis, breath is more vital to our existence than the constant chatter we pass off as thinking. We can live without thinking, but not without breathing. (Maybe Descartes should have said, "I breathe, therefore I am.")

Linking my awareness to my breath gave me a new sense of ease, calm, and integration with my body. Still, after several more meditation retreats, I began to see that I was not my thinking mind *or* my breath. I was awareness itself; a blank slate of consciousness. After I became more identitified with this quality of pure awareness, I could sit in meditation and watch, with complete acceptance, as all manner of phenomena appeared and disappeared. And none of it was me. This experience took place only in my deepest meditation periods, but nonetheless gave me a completely new perspective on who I think I am.

> *Americans cling to the myth of individualism as though it were the only normal way to live, unaware that it was unknown in the Middle Ages and would have been considered psychotic in classical Greece.*
>
> ROLLO MAY, *THE CRY FOR MYTH*

It is appropriate that Westerners, a group with the most highly developed sense of self in history, would finally turn to the East for help in diminishing it. Too much individuality is a burden—the individual is always competing, can never be good enough, never find enough love or security, never understand the source of his or her dissatisfaction. Excessive individuality is not good for the planet either; it saps our sense of responsibility to our communities, and to the rest of life as well.

Meditation takes us out of our own drama and allows us to identify ourselves as human and then, beyond that, as part of nature. It is a process of developing not only cosmic consciousness, but also species and biological consciousness. Seeing ourselves as part of these larger processes leads to a kind of radical humility, which I believe is the foundation of spirituality. The goal is to recognize that life is much greater and more mysterious than we can ever know, let alone control, and our biggest delusion is that we are separate from it all. These realizations can lead to empathy for it all, and love. As the Dalai Lama put it, summing up Tibetan Buddhism, "The view is interdependence. The action is compassion."

> *Once man is set to the pursuit of external things, he is never satisfied, as experience shows, with the mere necessities of life, but always strives after more and more, which, true to his predjudices, he always seeks in external things. Certainly, the external life of man can bear many improvements and beautifications, but they lose their significance to the extent to which the inner man cannot keep up with them. The provision with all "necessities" is, without doubt, a source of happiness which is not to be underestimated. But above and beyond it, the inner man raises his claim, which cannot be satisfied by any external goods: and the less this voice is heard in the hunt for "the wonderful things" of this world, the more the inner man becomes a source of inexplicable bad luck and understandable unhappiness in the midst of conditions of life from which one would expect something quite different. It is this which forms the illness of the Westerner, and he does not rest till he has infected the whole world with his greedy restlessness.*

CARL JUNG

The more I meditated, the more I became convinced it was a political act, a kind of personal sit-in. The third of Buddha's four noble truths states that happiness comes only by gaining control over one's mind, by diminishing our habits of desire rather than constantly trying to fulfill them. This truth would hold for our civilization as well as ourselves. In some way, learning that each moment is enough is a cure for our greedy restlessness, and also a rejection of consumerism and aggression.

Similarly, Mahatma Ghandi said the political and the spiritual could not be separated, and in *Earth House Hold*, which I read in 1971 after my first trip to India, Gary Snyder wrote "The mercy of the West has been social revolution; the mercy of the East has been individual insight into the basic self/void. We need both."

We haven't had both. Our culture has been so caught up in the drama of human history that we have lost touch with the forces that operate beyond us and through us. Meanwhile, our secular religions, communism and capitalism, have focused on the production and consumption of material wealth as the key to individual and societal happiness. Lip service is paid to other values, but only money talks.

> *Money is the visible deity, the transformation of all*
> *human and natural qualities into their opposite,*
> *the universal confusion and inversion of things.*
>
> KARL MARX

Adam Smith said the basis of free market capitalism is "enlightened self-interest." Unfortunately, very few capitalists are enlightened. In fact, the treadmill of capitalism is discontent; the whole system depends on stimulating endless desire. In Hinduism and Buddhism, however, the last stage of enlightenment is sometimes called *nirvana*, which literally means "the flames of desire have been extinquished." In other words, to many people enlightened self-interest is a contradiction in terms.

Communism, based on the sharing of resources, has its own built-in contradictions. Most people don't seem to be willing to sacrifice any of their own wealth for the common good. All the sharing in communist societies has therefore had to be politically enforced. This necessitates a ruling elite that inevitably succumbs to greed and corruption. Selfless sharing is a wonderful ideal, but first one has to get one's self out of the way.

To paraphrase Shakespeare, the fault, dear Brutus, lies not in our economic systems, but in ourselves. In the final analysis, uncontrolled desire, made worse by ignorance of what will truly make us happy, are the root of the problem. It's an affliction we all share.

One day while sitting in meditation in Bodhgaya, I began thinking about the war in Vietnam and the political struggles back home. Suddenly the face of President Nixon appeared in my mind. I had long felt a deep revulsion for Nixon, blaming him for the ongoing death and suffering in Vietnam and for the defeat of my generation's dreams. Now, though, all I could see was his suffering. I saw the tension in his squinting eyes and his short, stiff neck, the hunched and beleaguered shoulders ill-made to carry the load he had taken on. I felt the torment inside his mind, so full of worries and fears and convoluted schemes. A wave of compassion washed through me as I saw Nixon as no different from myself: deeply conditioned by his life circumstances, tortured by his desire to succeed and be loved. Tricky Dick, wherever you are now, I'm sorry for you and for all of us.

Through meditation, I came to perceive that there is no evil in the world, and no one to blame. We are all stuck on the same plateau of evolution, sharing the ills of a collective unconsciousness. I began to, as the Tibetan Buddhists say, "roll all blames into one."

> *Drinking a cup of green tea*
> *I stop the war.*
>
> PAUL REPS

All these personal and political insights were not what I'd expected to get out of meditation. When I first started sitting, what I really wanted was to experience the bliss of mystical Oneness. Many of the Westerners I met in India had similar exotic ideas about where a given spiritual practice would lead. We were after nothing less than everything, as usual.

Back in the '60s, hippies would sometimes break off a conversation by saying, "Well, everything is everything." That was a conversation-stopper for sure, but it also reflected a new understanding that all things are, indeed, connected. When we got to the East, however, the gurus told us that it doesn't matter if you *know* about cosmic unity; only merging with the One will end your suffering and change your life. Most of us agreed wholeheartedly with this prescription. Once inside the Oneness, we would lose our narrow, anthropomorphic worldviews and our painful self-consciousness. Furthermore, nirvana would kick in and the bliss would begin.

After two decades of meditation practice, I realize that getting into the One can be extremely difficult, and staying there is nigh on impossible. First of all, the path is full of paradoxes. For example, this special place that mystics have traditionally gone to is, in fact, where we are already. Trying to become one with the One is like playing musical chairs with yourself. Furthermore, in spite of the fact that there's nowhere to go, you've still got to make some effort or you'll never know that you are already there. And besides, once you get there, you aren't there. The One may be nice, but nobody's home.

If you're considering a journey into the One, here's my advice: First, decide what you want to call it, in case you get lost and need to ask directions. Most mystics agree that the One is indescribable, but they've given it many, many names, such as the Tao, "the isness," or—one of my favorites—"the unnameable." Jack Kerouac wrote, "I call it the golden eternity but you can call it anything you want." I like the Zen term "suchness," which has a funky, down-home kind of ring to it. "I'm just going out on the front porch for a spell, folks, to sit around in the good ol' suchness." When confronted with a nasty twist of fate though, I usually say to myself, "That's just the business of the isness."

At times, the One has been called "the unborn," but that term seems too loaded these days from its use in the abortion debate; it's also been called "the unmade," but that sounds like a bed. Other names include: the predicateless primordial essence, the imperishable, the source, the ground of being, the transcendent fullness of the emptiness (have yourself a waltz with that paradox), the dissolver of space and time and sangsaric mind, the weaver of the web of appearances, and last but not least, the outbreather and the inbreather of infinite universes throughout the endlessness of duration.

Modern physics has added a few new names for the One, such as "the space-time continuum." That's almost mantra quality, if you hold the "...uum." Another recent label is new-paradigm physicist David Bohm's "implicate order," a kind of cosmic pattern hidden inside of everything. It sounds to me like just another name for the Holy Ghost or the Buddhist Dharmakhaya.

I sometimes refer to the One as "the big everything" or "the big nothing," depending on my mood. It's difficult, however, to establish a relationship to abstractions such as these, and almost impossible to worship them. That's why most people give the One a face and personality. They want their metaphysics to be user-friendly. Enter the gods and goddesses. Humans seem to enjoy having a personal creator to adorn and adore, or even to curse and beseech. Brahma, Isis, Astarte, Allah, Jehovah, and Jesus are among the agents we have chosen to conduct our business with the Bureau of the Big Mystery. Each of them might be viewed as a stand-in for Oneness, a stunt-person for the big everything. And isn't it interesting, folks, that most of our gods and goddesses seem to end up looking a lot like ourselves. "Vanity of vanities," sayeth the Preacher. "All is vanity."

Unfortunately, people are always claiming to have found the *exclusive* name for the One. Trying to market this special name is probably the second-oldest human profession, and a few groups of people have made a fortune in the name-of-god business (have you ever been to the Vatican, or Bangkok's Emerald Wat?). Many more have fought wars, slaughtered, enslaved, and tortured others, all because they had different names for the supreme being. "Nyaah, nyaah! Our god's the real One, and your god's a false One" has been the battle cry of the ages. Sometimes people even kill each other in the name of the very same god, which must make it hard for the diety in question to take sides.

Many modern seekers have become alienated from all that god business, and have turned instead to the bare, amythical essence of everything.

By rejecting all the agents, or at least putting them on hold, we are exploring ways to have a direct, unmediated experience of ultimate reality. No more second-hand gods! No more worn-out metaphors! We want the One and we want it now!

> *And so, what is—or what is to be—the new mythology? It is—and will forever be, as long as our human race exists— the old, everlasting, perennial mythology, in its "subjective sense," poetically renewed in terms neither of a remembered past nor of a projected future, but of now: addressed, that is to say, not to the flattery of "peoples," but to the waking of individuals in the knowledge of themselves, not simply as egos fighting for place on the surface of this beautiful planet, but equally as centers of Mind at Large—each in his own way at one with all...*
>
> JOSEPH CAMPBELL, *MYTHS TO LIVE BY*

I returned from my first trip to India filled with great enthusiasm for meditation. Not wanting my mother to worry that I was praying to a new God named Buddha, I told her I had been studying psychology, which wasn't far from the truth. I had simply been trying to heal my confused mind. As a bottom line, the Buddha said, "All that we are arises with our thoughts. With our thoughts we make the world."

Meanwhile, back in San Francisco, some of my radical friends asked me, "How could you go shut your eyes and meditate while the slaughter is going on in Vietnam?" I tried to explain, babbling to them about a revolution in consciousness.

Soon after my return, I went back to work at KSAN doing news features and commentaries. I was determined to communicate the joys of Buddhist meditation to the counterculture, and, yes, change the world. I believed that if everyone on the planet would just sit and meditate for an

hour a day, peace would break out and we would all live happily ever after. A similar fantasy was the hippie notion that if everyone dropped acid,
love would rule the planet. Since neither experiment has been tried, we
still don't know whether or not they would work.

My missionary zeal was soon deflated. The problem turned out to be
more a matter of rhythm than content. When my slow, meditative messages came on the air in the middle of a set of rock and roll music, the radio station's energy would drop—pulse rate, decibels, and ratings. In
order to stay on the air, I turned up my internal speed until I was back in
sync with the rest of the culture. My radio broadcasts became popular
again, but my peace of mind began to dissipate. The speed and intensity
of our culture made it hard for me to sustain a strong mental focus, and
as a result, my perspective kept fading out.

Not that I gave up on meditation. In fact, as I again confronted the
sorry state of the world—as a journalist and a concerned human being. I
became even more convinced that the spiritual and political are one, and
that a transformation of consciousness was necessary to any revolution
worthy of the name. As Albert Einstein once said, "No problem can be
solved from the same consciousness that created it."

THE EVOLUTION OF THE REVOLUTION

Chapter Eight

When I returned from my second journey to India in 1973, I found the sixties' counterculture coming apart. Without the Vietnam War to hold it together, the peace and love movement had splintered into various sects, each going off to pursue its own dream and/or figure out new ways to subvert the dominant paradigm.

People cite a number of different dates as the end of that time known as "the sixties," depending on when their own package of revolutionary ideals and freeform lifestyle was squashed by the weight of the world. For some, the sixties ended at the Rolling Stones concert at Altamont in 1969, the day the good vibrations died. For others it was the killing of four Kent State University students by National Guard troops in the spring of 1970. Most of my own hippie hopes came to an end in 1972 when the American people reelected Richard Nixon for a second term. I realized then that the revolution would have to wait a while, and perhaps be conducted in more subtle ways.

And so it was. Some people went off to find nirvana or get rebirthed, others formed organizations to save the whales and redwoods or protect the entire planet. Quite a few joined sex- or gender-specific movements: gay, lesbian, women's, and men's. Many eased their way back into mainstream American society, often justifying their reentry by saying they were planning to subvert the system from within. Others blatantly started chasing the American dream again. The sixties had been a heady mix of idealism and indulgence, and white, middle-class revolutionaries seemed to drop back in as easily as they had dropped out.

I sold out quite a bit myself during the '70s and early '80s, at least according to the politically correct standards of a '60s radical. I did radio commercials for tennis shoes, computers, and once, even cellular car phones. I agonized over that ad, because the last thing I wanted was for people to feel more at home in their automobiles. But as the ancient saying goes, I needed the money.

Many of my Berkeley friends who had been political activists went into the food business, strange as that may seem. Some of them started a co-op called the Cheese Board; others opened restaurants and catering services. Instead of the planned-for social revolution, they ended up creating California cuisine. In one brief decade they went from radical to radicchio.

Of course, I too indulged a bit in the lifestyle that I continued to criticize on the radio as excessive. I'm no Gandhi. My style of living has, for the most part, fallen somewhere between hippie and yuppie. Let's call it "huppy." (Don't worry, be huppy.) Still, I didn't hand in my counterculture card at the lifestyle store. In my own bubble of otherness, I was convinced that America had lost its way, and that the world was going to hell in a paper and/or plastic bag. Luckily, I was living in Northern California, surrounded by people who saw things the same way.

On the radio throughout the '70s, I mainly covered the meandering streams of the counterculture and the decline of the American Empire. I still poked at the nation's military fixation and its consumer addictions, but my tone was much less strident than it had been during the Vietnam War.

For some reason, perhaps partly because of my Buddhist training,

I often found myself trying to ease my listeners' fears. (We teach what we need to learn.) One tactic I used was to begin my broadcasts by reminding people to keep the news in a larger perspective, to "step into a bigger frame than what each day's events proclaim." The introduction to my broadcasts became a kind of cosmic disclaimer to the news:

> *The little blue-green planet spins endlessly on its*
> *axis, causing the lifeforms that live on the surface*
> *to become dizzy and bump into each other, creat-*
> *ing* news. *And here is a report on some of the colli-*
> *sions for Wednesday, November 19th....*

I also tried to cover the latest scientific theories and discoveries: news of quarks and quasars, parallel universes and galaxy clusters. Focusing occasionally on the impersonal forces of physics and astronomy can, I believe, be a balm of no little measure. At least, working on these stories made me feel better. As I told my journalist friends, "You are what you cover." Besides, in the '70s we needed all the perspectives we could find.

> *The future is a misted landscape, no man*
> *sees clearly, but at cyclic turns*
> *There is a change felt in the rhythm of events, as when*
> *an exhausted horse*
> *Falters and recovers, then the rhythm of the running*
> *hoofbeats is changed: he will run miles yet,*
> *But he must fall: we have felt it again in our own lifetime,*
> *slip, shift, and speed up*
> *In the gallop of the world; and now perceive that, come*
> *peace or war, the progress of Europe and America*
> *Becomes a long process of deterioration—starred with*
> *famous Byzantiums and Alexandrias,*
> *Surely—but downward. One desires at such times*

To gather the insights of the age summit against future
loss, against the narrowing mind and the tyrants
The pedants, the mystagogues, the barbarians...

ROBINSON JEFFERS, "PRESCRIPTION OF PAINFUL END"

I had returned from India to a country in deep crisis. In 1973, the United States was withdrawing from Vietnam, morally and militarily defeated, under the cover of a euphemism called "Vietnamization." As the war wound down, a recession began at home, cutting into the radicals and hippies' ability to live cheaply on the edges of society, and into America's tolerance for any behavior that deviated from the norm. The decade's mood was set in 1973 with the onset of the so-called energy crisis, which also began to define a new counterculture struggle with American society.

The problem started when oil-rich nations, mostly around the Arabian peninsula, got together to form OPEC, the Organization of Petroleum Exporting Countries, or, as I called them on KSAN, the O'peckers. This coalition suddenly decided to tie a knot in their big gas hose to the West until we cried uncle and forked over more money. This was a serious challenge to our icon, the automobile, the symbol of our freedom to go wherever we wanted, whether around the block or halfway 'round the planet to get the gas to go around the block.

Many people in the nascent environmental movement saw the energy crisis as a positive development, a way to slow down the juggernaut called progress and curtail the rape of the planet. As Stewart Brand, the editor of the *Whole Earth Catalog*, told me in a 1973 radio interview, "We're in a race between a biological collapse and an economic collapse. I'm cheering for the economic collapse to come in first."

I agreed that the energy crisis was a good idea—at least when I wasn't caught in a long line at a gas station. In California we could only get gas on alternative days, determined by whether your car's license plate ended in an odd or even number. I was thankful to be able to say, "I'm odd."

My Buddhist training had led me to believe that our civilization's

The Evolution of the Revolution

speed was its fatal flaw. In meditation I learned how much harder it is to be aware of what you are doing when you are moving fast. I remain convinced that the real energy crisis is our hyperactivity, and that the next revolution will be a slowdown. Consciousness may be the ultimate speed bump.

Looking back, I realize that another kind of energy cartel should have been formed in the 1970s, and still could be today. Oil is not the only dark-colored liquid vital to the functioning of the techno-industrialized world. Consider the various forms of caffeine that fuel the workforce's nervous systems as surely as the oil fuels their machines. The coffee-and tea-growers of the world could hold the industrialized economies hostage by joining together into a Caffeine Producing and Exporting Cartel, or CAPEX. ("Listen up, America. It's either CAPEX, or Caffix.") It would be made up of Juan Valdez and his fellow Columbian coffee growers, and all the nameless workers in Brazil and Sumatra and Kenya, along with the tea growers of India, Sri Lanka, and China—all those impoverished people who for generations have broken their backs picking beans and tearing leaves off bushes only to sell them for next to nothing to Liptons and Twinings and Folgers and General Foods so that we could stimulate our nervous systems to a sufficiently high pitch to conquer the world and henceforth control the price of coffee and tea. CAPEX's number one demand should be that Western people relax a little.

> *During the Industrial Revolution all but one of the seven deadly sins, sloth, was transformed into a positive virtue. Greed, avarice, envy, gluttony, luxury, and pride were the driving forces of the new economy.*
>
> LEWIS MUMFORD, *TRANSFORMATION OF MAN*

Only after one civilization matures can another be born. Oswald Spengler mapped out the lifecycles of all world cultures in his classic study, *The Decline of the West*: imperialism, he says, is the final stage, and also the time when the seeds of something new begin to grow within the mother country. Perhaps the late-twentieth-century American subcultures will be as influential as those of pre-Socratic Greece, or the Christian cults during the Roman Empire. Maybe, however, they are just a late Romantic movement, made up of sentimentalists trying to hold on to a quickly receding world. History will decide.

One subculture that seems likely to thrive, in all its political and religious expressions, is environmentalism. As human society increasingly bumps up against the earth's limitations, our instinct for self-preservation should turn us back to nature. The movement is taking the form of gritty political battles over wilderness and biodiversity, as well as the spread of neo-pagan rituals and the new wholistic paradigm. A revival of nature worship is only to be expected, given the nature of our times.

I first heard the word "ecology" from a hippie named Keith Lampe, who began publishing a newsletter in the late '60s called *Earth Read Out* (Lampe later changed his name to Ponderosa Pine and fell in love with a woman who called herself Olive Tree.) One day in the fall of 1969, Lampe called me at KSAN to report that the air in Berkeley had become too polluted for him to do his yogic breathing in the park.

Environmental issues started becoming front-page news a little later, around the time that the first U.N. Conference on the Environment was held in Stockholm, in 1972. A lot of people I knew from San Francisco went to that conference, but, as might be expected, only to protest outside of the official meetings. My friends saw the environmental crisis as far more severe and widespread than any government had yet acknowledged. Gary Snyder wrote:

No one came to the 1972 U.N. Conference on the Environment to give anything—they all came to take. Not to save the planet, but to argue about how to divide it up and stretch it out—how to prolong the agony. People thought and spoke in terms of political divisions and human needs. No one spoke for the actual biological and ethnic zones of the planet, and the interrelated needs of all beings. No one except for the Hopi Indian delegation.

GARY SNYDER, *NEW DIRECTIONS #26*

Some California hippies took a life-size gray-whale-shaped balloon to the Stockholm conference to gain publicity for a proposed ban on whaling. Whales were the first environmental mascot. There have been others since then—the proud bald eagle and the cute baby harp seal—but it was the barnacled blowhard, the biggest creature on the planet that captured this first wave of eco-activists' imaginations.

I was involved with the whale campaign as both radio newscaster and advocate, and in 1976 was asked to fly to Japan with a music show called the Dolphin Project. The idea was to put on a big rock-and-roll concert and simultaneously educate Japanese kids about the plight of whales and dolphins. Performers included Jackson Browne, Ritchie Havens, Warron Zevon, Odetta, John Sebastian, Danny O'Keefe, Wavy Gravy, and many others. The never-say-die hippies believed that rock-and-roll could help save whales, just as it had helped to shorten the Vietnam war.

Young Japanese jammed the Tokyo concert hall to hear the music, but they seemed indifferent to the whale exhibits set up on the perimeter of the auditorium. Interviewing people waiting in line for the show, I asked one Japanese kid why he had come. He replied, "To see Mister John Sebastian sing his song from *Welcome Back Kotter.* "And how do you feel about the whales?" I asked. "Oh, the whales," he said, smiling enthusiastically, "they are very delicious."

By the late 1970s, the environmental movement had taken on Noah's project, trying to save all species of life. Some who took part were conservationists who believed that biodiversity is necessary for human survival; others, adherents of "deep ecology," were simply struggling for the inalienable right of all species to life, liberty, and the pursuit of happiness. Those who put the issue in political terms, sometimes called nonhuman species "the fifth world." But the movement was more than political. It was a pagan call, harkening people back to nature.

On the autumnal equinox in 1978, I covered the First Annual All Species Gathering and Celebration at San Francisco's Civic Center Plaza. The local pagan environmentalists attended this event dressed as their totem plants and animals, in their finest furs, feathers, scales, bark, and shells, accessorized with horns, tusks, plumes, manes, tails, fins, and leaves. Even dragons and unicorns showed up to warn that mythological beings are endangered by human disregard and forgetfulness, and that losing these fantasy species would diminish the stories and wonder that are essential to life.

I came in a wolf mask, and told the other species that I was a pack journalist on the prowl for a good story. My favorite interview that day was with a man completely covered in strips of bamboo that tinkled when he walked. He said he represented Bapi Bapi, the ancient African spirit of bamboo, and informed me that the first music heard on earth was the wind playing across a bamboo forest.

There were rituals and ceremonies throughout the day, and each species had a chance to speak, bark, sound, cry, growl, chirp, laugh (a hyena was present), or whoop. The whoops came from several whooping cranes who announced that there were only 105 of their kind left in the world, and it was getting harder to find anyone with whom to make whoopie.

In 1984, a similar group of species representatives gathered outside the Democratic National Convention in San Francisco. Hardly any of the convention delegates came outside to hear what they had to say, but a lot of press showed up. I remember watching one Canadian T.V. reporter who had the audacity to walk right into the middle of a ritual to deliver his on-camera wrap-up. Planting himself directly in front of a giant bald eagle who was chanting the names of endangered bird species, this reporter, with a concerned look on his face, intoned, "Antics like these from the lunatic fringe here in San Francisco just might give the Democrats a bad image in this year's presidential election race."

Behind the anchorman, the bald eagle continued to sing out the names of those facing extinction: "eight species of crane, five species of duck, twelve species of parrot, twenty species of pheasant, three species of doves, three species of hawk, four species of owl, the Canadian goose, the African ostrich, the Chinese egret, the red-cockaded woodpecker...."

> *It's time to make people more important than owls.*
>
> GEORGE BUSH, CAMPAIGN SPEECH, SEPTEMBER, 1992

I was shocked when I actually read the current list of endangered species. It's like a Who's Who of the natural world, full of lions and tigers and elephants and songbirds and butterflies, all our favorites from the television nature shows, from our dreams and nightmares, our fables and poetry.

This list could be read as a major indictment of human civilization, equivalent to the charges at Nuremburg. Some biologists now estimate that we are losing 27,000 species every year—seventy-four each day, three every hour. Why aren't the bells tolling day and night? Shouldn't the list be read aloud in churches and schools, updated regularly on the front pages of newspapers? Whenever a species is added to the list, maybe its picture should appear on milk cartons.

I think our paradigm is the problem. For instance, we like to make a distinction between "natural" disasters, and those caused by humans. That's because we think of ourselves as removed from nature. But we are indeed part of nature, and as such, *we are a natural disaster*—like a violent hurricane or plague of locusts moving across the planet. Humanity's impact on the course of evolution may be as significant as that of the meteorite that supposedly ended the reign of the dinosaurs. Meanwhile, scientists do not even think about putting humans on the endangered species list yet. They still believe that a species is endangered only when there are too *few* of its kind.

These days we hear the cry of Eeek! connecting everything on the material plane. Eeek!-cology. Eeek!-conomy. Amer-eek!-a. And the free-eeks! Eeek! Eeek! Eeeeeek...

INTRODUCTION TO ONE OF MY KSAN NEWSCASTS, 1976

In the late 1960s, I used to play a brief cut from the Broadway show *Brecht on Brecht* as a comment on the news. Lotte Lenya, in her thick German accent, read Brecht on Europe in the 1930s: "I live in a time of darkness indeed. A harmless word is absurd, a smooth brow suggests indifference. He who laughs has not yet received the frightful news. What times are these, when a talk about trees is almost criminal. It means one does not talk about the crimes."

By the late '70s, people were talking about the trees *and* the crimes in the same breath, especially the destruction of the rainforests. I remember how astonished I was to hear that the tropical forests were being cut down so that cattle ranchers could supply fast-food hamburgers to the industrialized world. Cows had already laid waste the grasslands and waterways of the Western U.S., now they were trampling the tropics as well.

I imagined a horror movie called *The Hamburger That Ate the Amazon*, in which a giant hamburger bun attacks the rainforest, opening and closing like a huge mouth, gobbling up trees and animals and native tribes. The spilled blood of Indians and anacondas and alligators pours out of the sides of the bun like ketchup, and the lush jungle foliage protrudes as the garnish.

We have recently discovered that eating cows is not even good for us. Cow meat and cow milk fill the human blood stream with deadly fats.

Even worse, cow farts are a major cause of ozone depletion. The cows are getting their revenge. Americans have always eaten hamburger and steak with pride, but maybe for our bodily and planetary salvation we should now adopt the Hindu idea of "holy cow."

In the late 1970s, the struggle against nuclear power became the environmental movement's Vietnam War. After seeing what happened at Hiroshima and Nagasaki, many of my generation were extremely sensitive to the threat of nuclear radiation. We could not believe that our politicians and business leaders would make a Faustian bargain with the deadliest poison ever known. This was the primal fire, and, like Prometheus, if we messed with it the gods would order birds to eat out our livers while we were still alive.

In an astonishing feat of hubris, the scientists and corporate executives had convinced each other, and much of the public as well, that they could contain the toxic waste for hundreds of thousands of years to come. What many of us found even more outrageous was the fact that this risk was being taken largely to fuel more mindless consumption.

My radio show at the time featured my satirist friend Darryl Henriques's rapid-fire ninety-second commercial for a product that we claimed would solve all of America's energy problems:

Are you worried about the energy crisis? Disgusted with high utility bills? Fed up with being an energy victim? Then take control of your life today and make your home energy self-sufficient with U.S. Atom's Home Nuclear Reactor. Small enough to fit into your abandoned fallout shelter yet powerful enough to power your major home appliances, including your washer, dryer, stove, refrigerator, freezer, microwave, waffle iron, toaster, coffeemaker, mixer, blender, food processor, Crockpot™, electric wok, electric knife, knife sharpener, can opener, popcorn popper, cheese grater, meat slicer, dishwasher, garbage dis-

posal, trash compactor, electric broom, vacuum cleaner, water heater, hot tub, sauna, Water Pik™, electric toothbrush, alarm clock, AM-FM radio, tape deck, turntable, amplifier, color television, VCR, electric lights, and your automatic garage-door opener. Not to mention dad's electric typewriter, skill saw, table saw, chain saw, edge and edge trimmer, and mom's sewing machine, steam iron, curling iron, hair dryer, and vibrator, your son's electric guitar, amp, preamp, eco-plex, and wah-wah pedal, and your daughter's electric disco party dress. Your home nuclear reactor comes fully equipped with a lightweight plastic containment vessel and easy-to-follow emergency instructions in case of a mini meltdown. If you order today, you'll receive free directions on how to assemble a home-size atom bomb out of your leftover nuclear wastes, enabling you to become a dominant military power in your very own neighborhood. Join the millions who will soon go nuclear with U.S. Atom's Home Nuclear Reactor. Get 'em while they're hot!

In California, the nuclear power struggle centered around the Diablo Canyon Nuclear Reactor, a name that was a nightmare for Pacific Gas and Electric's public relations department, but fit perfectly into the symbolic arsenal used by the antinuclear forces. Here was the techno-devil himself, holding the lethal poison inside two gleaming-steel futuristic domes built on the idyllic coastal hills of Southern California.

During the protests, I interviewed a Native American of the Chumash tribe, whose ancestors buried their dead on the site where the nuclear power plant was built. He seemed eager to speak, saying "These corporate people don't understand that the dead are not powerless. At least the Spanish conquerors heeded our warning and didn't build anything in that canyon. After all, the Spanish are the ones who named it 'Diablo.' Even they knew enough not to mess around in there."

Power company officials did not seem to care that they might be arousing the spirits of the dead, but they *were* hard-pressed to justify building a nuclear reactor just a few miles from an active earthquake fault. That was surely tempting the devil.

The protests at Diablo Canyon were great ritual theater. At one major rally, affinity groups from all over the Western states gathered at the plant's main gate. After chanting praises to the sun, each group climbed the fence to perform some symbolic action or ceremony before being arrested for trespassing. A group called Sympathy for the Devil performed a scene from King Lear before they were handcuffed and led away. One group from Mendocino County, called the White Egrets, leaped the fence to plant California poppy seeds and Monterey pine trees. Wavy Gravy, the omnipresent counterculture clown, brought a group called (and dressed as) the Mutant Sponges.

What took place at Diablo Canyon was as much exorcism as political protest, not unlike the Yippies' attempt to levitate the Pentagon in the '60s. But the tactics failed. Diablo was given a full operating license and today sits waiting on the fault line.

The antinuclear movement's fears were justified in late March of 1979 when a cooling system malfunctioned at Unit 2 of the Three Mile Island nuclear reactor in Pennsylvania, causing a partial core meltdown and the release of some radioactive material into the environment. Pregant women and children were evacuated from a five-mile radius of the plant, but all other area residents were told by a spokesperson from the Pennsylvania Governor's office, "Just stay inside your houses and keep your windows shut." That was excellent advice—but only for those who had houses made of lead.

The partial meltdown at Three Mile Island energized the antinuclear movement for a big march on Washington, D.C., on May 6th, 1979, which I covered for KSAN news. Dr. Barry Commoner may have been reaching too hard for history that day when he announced to the crowd, "As of today, the nuclear age has died, and the solar age is born." (Some readers may remember that in the late '70s there was a lot of talk about solar energy, renewable resources, appropriate technologies, and lowered expectations, ideas that somehow got lost in the corporate shuffle of the '80s.)

Comedian-activist Dick Gregory, too, miscalculated the significance of that day in Washington. A decade earlier, Gregory had vowed not to eat any solid foods until the Vietnam War was over, and now he told the crowd that he would fast until every nuclear power plant in America was closed down.

I remember Gregory telling the crowd that nuclear radiation was the most dangerous enemy they would ever have to face. He said, "I can see war, I can feel racism, I can feel hunger. But I cannot *see* radiation, I cannot *smell* radiation, I cannot *feel* radiation." He told the protestors to go back to their communities and "make radiation real!" Seemingly in response to that call, Allen Ginsberg wrote a poem entitled "Plutonian Ode":

> *O heavy heavy Element awakened I vocalize your*
> *consciousness to six worlds*
> *I chant your absolute Vanity. Yeah monster of Anger*
> *birthed in fear O most*
> *Ignorant matter ever created unnatural to Earth! Delusion*
> *of metal empires!*
> *Destroyer of lying Scientists! Devourer of covetous*
> *Generals, Incinerator of Armies and Melter of Wars!*
> *Judgment of judgments, Divine Wind over vengeful*
> *nations, Molestor of Presidents, Death-Scandal of*
> *Capital politics! Ah civilization stupidly industrious!*
> *Canker-Hex on multitudes learned or illiterate!*
> *Manufactured Spectre of human reason! O solidified*
> *imago of practitioners in Black Arts*
> *I dare your reality, I challenge your very being! I*
> *publish your cause and effect!*
>
> FROM "PLUTONIAN ODE"

The environmental movement that emerged in the 1970s is perhaps more deeply rooted in Northern California than anywhere else on the planet. While visiting the region in 1911, philosopher George Santayana wrote to a friend, "I am struck here by the deep and almost religious affection which people have for nature...It is their spontaneous substitute for articulate art and articulate religion."

Following the lead of John Muir, the Northern California environmental movement grew along with environmental degredation, although never quite keeping pace. It coalesced in mid-century under the banner of Bay Area organizations such as the Sierra Club and, later, Friends of the Earth, and expanded in the 1980s with the formation of Earth Island Institute and the Rainforest Action Network. Greenpeace and Earth First! recruited many of their eco-warriors from Northern California, as ex-beatniks and hippies *and their children* signed up to save the planet.

The Sierra Club developed a powerful lobby and eventually moved its headquarters to Washington D.C., Earth First! sent its troops to chain themselves to thousand-year-old redwood trees, and Greenpeace members took to the high seas to confront whalers and ships transporting nuclear materials. And while these activists (and their lawyers) fought the physical and political battles, Bay Area eco-philosophers were developing eco-theories and writing books about a whole new worldview.

In the early 1980s, I was invited to join the Elmwood Institute in Berkeley, a "new paradigm" think tank. Elmwood was the brainchild of Fritjof Capra, author of *The Tao of Physics* and *The Turning Point*. Its members are trying to come up with a new Western ethos that includes the feminine and nature and other cultures under its heaven. Members include Ernest Callenbach, author of *Ecotopia*, Jerry Mander, who wrote *Four Arguments for the Elimination of Television* and *In the Absence of the Sacred*, Joanna Macy, author of *Despair and Empowerment in the Nuclear Age* and *World As Lover, World As Self*, and Charlene Spretnack, author of *Lost Goddesses of Early Greece* and *Green Politics*.

Out here on the Pacific Coast fault lines, these friends of mine are trying to shift a paradigm as heavy as a continent. Their own worldview is a patchwork of modern systems theory and quantum physics, interlaced with ancient Taoist ideas about nature and the old Buddhist concept of "dependent co-arising." It's the all-new ancient ways. Many of the Elmwood group would number themselves among the deep ecologists, who understand the earth itself as a single living organism—sometimes referred to as a goddess named Gaia. Rather than the crown of creation, humanity is often seen as a thorn in her side.

The Elmwood Institute thinkers are helping to build a theoretical foundation for environmentalism, the new radical political ideology. From their perspective, communism and capitalism are just two different methods of organizing the takeover of the third, fourth, and fifth worlds. The Cold War was simply a struggle for the right to ravage the earth.

My Elmwood friends are opposed to bigness, whether in the form of nation states, corporations, or human population. Aside from trying to curtail human expansion, they feel their most urgent task is to resist the unchecked growth of technology—and its handmaiden, consumerism—which they see as mindlessly gobbling up the earth's resources and collapsing its ecosystems. At stake, they believe, is nothing less than life itself.

Rather than production and consumption, the measure of success for any human society is now sustainability—a level of economic activity that *the planet* can afford. That literally means a tapering off and eventual end to economic growth, a concept as unthinkable to most politicians and pundits as the elimination of sex or television. The alternative to continued growth—equally unthinkable to those in power—would be a real redistribution of wealth. At the risk of sounding sappy, one might also call it sharing.

My eco-philosopher friends are not only sounding the alarm, they are also offering alternatives. For example, former Haight-Ashbury organizer Peter Berg started an organization way back in the early 1970s called Planet Drum Foundation, which promotes a complete restructuring of Western society. Berg thinks nation-states ought to be broken up into "bioregions," based on climate and geographical boundaries, with populations united by their common natural surroundings. To form these bioregions, Berg calls for "reinhabitation," an alternative to our mobile, fragmented way of life. Reinhabitation simply means that people would settle down and live somewhere.

Berg wants us to put down roots and create communities. He encourages the growth of new "native" cultures out of the vast American sameness. Just as some environmentalists fear the loss of biodiversity, Berg warns against encroaching "monoculture" and the loss of cultural diversity. In 1976, the year of the American Bicentennial, Berg sent out a poetic broadside entitled "Ambling Towards Continental Congress," in which he proposed an unusual new coalition of peoples who exist beyond the boundaries of any nation-state:

> *Reinhabitants of North America see the bright colors of inhabitory people in tree-tiered Amazon jungles, ocean-spirited islands of Micronesia, dances of African forests and rivers; Basque, Breton, Provencal tongues revive to pronounce their places in Europe; share the affirmation of self-determination with delta-farmers in Southeast Asia, Yaponesian and Hokkaido Islanders, Altai Mountain nomads; feel the strength and seek the long-time vision of people native to the continent we are learning to share. There is a one-to-one balance between our own decentralized regional integrity and the survival of Kurdish mountain autonomy, Xingu jungle homeland, and Lapp reindeer range. There is the union of Earth's biosphere holding us in common, and the promise of human species consciousness to gain.*

Of course this can be seen as a romantic or nostalgic attempt to hold onto a lost world. But at least it offers another vision, something extremely rare in the public debate over our collective future. Berg's ideas—like most of my friends' work at Elmwood—have been largely ignored by the mainstream media, except when ridiculed. Their views are regarded as too strange, their prophecies and warnings too shrill or unrealistic. As a result, most people don't even hear of their wisdom, let alone heed it.

Maybe the vision of a funky, down-home, small-scale society is too "retro" for today's gleaming high-tech world. Furthermore, I'll admit that my friends and I sometimes indulge in a little sensationalism about the crisis, as well as sentimentalism about the solution. Still, when I read the news of growing ecological and social dysfunction, and then hear world leaders propose more economic growth and competition as the solution, I know that we are on the right path to the future.

U.S. Out of North America!

BUMPERSTICKER, 1976

Environmentalism may finally be bringing together the separate strands of the counterculture, ending the long-standing tension between the political left and the psycho-spiritual explorers. The split goes back to the '60s, when radicals accused hippies of being self-indulgent mystics, while hippies accused radicals of being stuck in outdated political forms.

One bizarre incident serves to illustrate this rift. In 1976, a group of political leftists in New York distributed a leaflet accusing the Dalai Lama of murdering Chairman Mao. The Dalai Lama had, indeed, performed a special Tibetan Buddhist ritual, the Kalachakra, on the very day that Mao died, and when the leftists heard about it, they decided to blame him for Mao's death. But some Americans who were studying Tibetan Buddhism quickly intervened. They called a press conference to announce that since Mao had died on the same day as the Kalachakra ceremony, he would be assured passage to the Buddha heaven. In other words, not only had the

Dalai Lama not murdered Chairman Mao, he may even have saved him a few million reincarnations. According to the Buddhists, the Maoists had been both politically and spiritually incorrect.

Today, many environmental activists will admit that some of the new psycho-spiritual practices are fueling a positive evolutionary energy. Reconnecting people with their bodies, diminishing ego through meditation, expanding individual identity to include community and nature, and even reviving pagan rituals—these are increasingly understood as the therapeutic and religious components of environmentalism.

Theodore Roszac, a Bay Area author who wrote the classic '60s treatise *Where the Wasteland Ends*, is currently formulating a new discipline called eco-psychology. Roszac frames his goal in *The Voice of the Earth*, where he writes, "Both the therapists and the ecologists offer us a common political agenda for the good of the planet, for the good of the person. It is simply stated: Scale down. Slow down. Democratize. Decentralize."

Eco-psychology has already been joined by a discipline called eco-spirituality. Of course, we also have eco-investing and eco-travel and eco-management and eco-art. Some of it is just eco-tripping, but at least that's better than ego-tripping. In fact, ego and eco may grow in inverse proportion to each other.

It's too soon to say whether environmentalism will succeed in popularizing this new worldview. It's only about twenty-five years old, after all, very young for a worldview. Back when it was just beginning to walk, sometime in 1976, Gary Snyder captured its ongoing counterculture spirit thus, during an interview on KSAN:

> *What we can only hope for is that the coming economic collapse does not tear the biology down with it as it goes. We have to help ease people's minds so that they are not so anxious about giving up some of their material wealth. The real danger is that the industrialized societies will*

consume every last shred of timber, every last scrap of wild meat, every last drop of oil, and leave the planet completely ravaged. The best thing that a person like myself can do is to communicate a joyful vision of the alternative, to help allay the fear, and smooth the turning to another direction.

I agree with most of what my eco-philosopher friends have to say, mostly because I would rather live in their future than the one towards which the world often seems headed. However, I really don't think they go far enough. We may be trying to save planet earth, but I believe we should also pay attention to the ecological health of the entire cosmos. After all, it's the only cosmos we've got. Maybe what we need is a more comprehenisve environmental philosophy, a deeper ecology. The currently popular Gaia hypothesis tells us that our planet is a single, living organism, but certainly the same can be said of the universe, which is one evolutionary process of matter-energy, growing into its skin of space-time.

Still, the Friends of the Earth seem strangely unconcerned, while Earth First! appears to ignore other galaxies and their possible life forms. Perhaps a new motto is needed: Universe First! Earth Second! You may object, "But you should be thinking locally!" Okay. Then let's start an organization called Friends of the Solar System, dedicated to having our immediate neigborhood in space declared a protected wilderness area. The rest of the planets should be set aside as a "Sky Park" and earthlings prohibited from colonizing or exploiting them. Already there are thousands of pieces of human-made debris orbiting around our planet. We must keep humans from further trashing the 'hood. (A good slogan would be: We Need Our Space!)

This is not just a gigantic metaphor. Physicists say an atomic event in one part of the universe is simultaneously felt everywhere else. The chaos theorists tell us that a butterfly's wings flapping in Yosemite may affect weather patterns on Alpha Centauri. On some very basic level, everything is truly connected. Gaia may have been goddess enough for the Greeks, but we need a deity whose arms can encompass vast clusters of galaxies, and our fantastic human imagination as well.

> *Do you think you can take over the universe and improve it? I do not believe it can be done.*
>
> TAO TE CHING

One side-benefit of participation in the new spiritual and environmental movements is the opportunity to celebrate a few extra holidays. Not only do I get to do Christmas and the 4th of July, I also sometimes gather with friends on the two solstices and equinoxes to feast and read poetry. In May I might choose to celebrate the Buddha's birthday, and in October walk with candles through the streets of San Francisco's Mission District to mark the Day of the Dead. I continue to celebrate Passover, but around our table Moses sometimes gets turned into a feminist, and the Buddha is usually brought in as a kind of "Moses of the mind."

Halloween, Mardi Gras, and Gay Pride Week are major holidays in San Francisco, and some irreverant ritualists have even created their own saints and festivals. One of my favorites is the annual Saint Stupid's Day Parade, which winds through the city's financial district every April 1st at noontime. Saint Stupid is the patron saint of parking meters and civilizations, and every year hundreds of people come downtown dressed as fools and clowns to honor him and receive his blessing. They usually bring a few extra socks with them, to be traded and thrown into the air during a ceremony in front of the Pacific Coast Sock Exchange. People are always happy to watch their socks go up. The celebrants are always promised a free lunch as well, but somehow it never seems to materialize.

Several corporations have actually tried to buy sponsorship of this parade, but the fools in charge refuse to tarnish the image of Saint Stupid.

Ho, Ho, Ho Chi Minh, NLF is gonna win.

ANTIWAR CHANT, 1968

Ho, Ho, Homosexual. Ruling class is ineffectual.

GAY RIGHTS CHANT, 1979

One of the most significant social events of the '70s, especially in San Francisco, was the gay and lesbian coming-out party. I observed it both through the lives of my gay and lesbian friends, and as a journalist in the mecca of gaydom, where I covered the parades and political conventions.

In fact, purely by accident, I was one of only three journalists to witness San Francisco's first Gay Freedom Day parade. The marchers happened to pass the KSAN studios, and someone ran up to tell me that some kind of demonstration was going by. I watched fifty or so gay men marching down the sidewalks of San Francisco's business district on that spring day in 1969, chanting and carrying a banner demanding "homosexual rights."

A small corps of campy baton twirlers led, and a few drag queens brought up the rear, causing businessmen to stare in shock and wonder. There were no lesbians in that first parade. Within ten years—by June of 1979—more than 300,000 people marched down Market Street, the city's main thoroughfare, celebrating their various lifestyles in the official, city-sponsored, "Lesbian and Gay Freedom Day Parade."

I covered most of these parades, and watched the evolution of traditions that are now as cherished as Lions Club ceremonies in other parts of America. For instance, the infamous Dykes on Bikes always lead the parades, riding in formation on their Harleys and Hondas, often bare-breasted, hair cut short, fists raised, laughing and shouting at the crowd. Many Jewish lesbians and gay men march together as "The Lost Tribe," while the members of the Gay Business Association march with individual signs, such as, "I'm a lawyer and I'm gay," "I'm a construction worker and I'm gay," or "I'm a librarian and I'm gay." Once I interviewed a man who carried a sign reading "I'm bourgeois and I'm gay." He told me he didn't want people to think that all gays were wild, left-wing crazies, because he certainly wasn't.

One of my parade favorites is the bunch of people who march together under the banner, "The Displaced Oakies." They sing, "Oklahoma, O-K-I'm-gay-oh-ho-I'm-gay, Oklahoma, I'm gay!" with great gusto. Steinbeck never imagined such a migration.

Even though I think of myself as a San Francisco veteran—someone who had seen a lot of unique behavior over the years—I am always shocked by *something* at the parades. One year I interviewed a contingent of sadomasochists who were finally "coming out." They marched in front of their own little float, a flatbed truck carrying two master-slave couples in leather harnesses, framed by big loud speakers blaring bass-heavy disco music. A big banner in front of the group read, "S & M... The Last Closet," and some of the marchers carried placards reading, "Black and Blue is Beautiful."

In recent years, the parades have been less exuberant because of the devastation of the AIDS epidemic, but the annual expression of sexual choice and cultural freedom continues. Unfortunately, the gays and lesbians still have a long way to march before being accepted in America. Their existence raises both spiritual and political hackles. They have to struggle to be seen not as sinners, and also as citizens.

During the mid-century social upheavals, I, too, had some difficulty with my personal life, as my own family kept coming apart and reforming. My parents had always assumed I would marry one of "our kind" (a Jew), remain monogomous, and raise children in the typical nuclear family. But sexual, moral, religious, and even technological revolutions intervened to destroy their hopes for me. Like most of my generation, I no longer could believe that God cared about sex outside of marriage, and birth control eliminated any other reason to abstain. Meanwhile, the mainstream culture promoted sex and romance as the ultimate experiences, and by the '70s the only ethic was, "If it feels good, do it."

Perhaps as a consequence, almost everyone I know has had two or three spouses, many lovers, and often several sets of children and step-children, creating all sorts of zig-zagging lines of relations and relationships. Sometimes it doesn't feel all that good, either.

By the mid '70s, my wife and I had separated several times. We finally decided to have a child in 1976 to see if that would solidify our bond. A year and a half later we split up for good. Maybe it was because Mudita (formerly Karol) required that I change every other diaper, and kept careful count. I may have thought I aspired to ultimate liberation back then, but I wasn't ready to be liberated from traditional gender roles.

After a couple of years of separation, Mudita and I became the best of friends. For my fortieth birthday she arranged a surprise party and hired a belly dancer to perform. I was immediately entranced, and eventually fell in love with the dancer, Teresa Vandiver, a nurse and a comrade in meditation. After ten years together we still can't quite figure out what to name our bond—are we partners, mates, lovers? Not so very long ago, people called it "living in sin."

Along the way, my daughter's childhood turned out to be as different from mine as mine was from my father's. Since the age of two, Rose has lived half the time with me and half with her mother. When she was three, I lived for a while in bohemian North Beach. Mornings I would push Rose in her stroller down Broadway, past the nightclubs and strip joints, to Caffe Trieste, where Mama Yolanda would give her a free glass of steamed milk.

When Rose was four, we moved into a communal house in Oakland, where we lived until she was fifteen. For a while in early adolescence, Rose was embarrased to tell her friends about her group living situation. In truth, however, she loved it. The commune was multigenerational, and Rose grew up with many doting "aunts" and "uncles," all related by choice.

For the sake of tradition and stability, I tried to give Rose a sense of her Jewish roots, even though I have pulled up many of my own. We celebrate Rosh Hashanah, Chanukah, and Passover, and she is familiar with the rituals and their meaning. But I was really thrilled when Rose decided on her own to get involved in Buddhist meditation. I felt like a Jewish father at his daughter's bas mitzvah, swelling with pride over her initiation into the Buddha's tribe, not Abraham's.

On the subject of cultural influences, I should add that Mudita plays in the Berkeley Balinese gamelon orchestra, and Rose started Balinese dance lessons when she was five. She eventually became the youngest Caucasian ever to perform Balinese dance in public. When my father came to San Francisco to see her performance, he was dazzled by the costumes and gong-rock music, and charmed by his grandaughter's skill. At one point during the dance, however, I caught my father's eye, and we simultaneously shook our heads in perplexed bemusement, a shared moment of wonder at the fact that our family of wandering Jews had traveled from Poland to Norfolk, Nebraska, to San Francisco, to Bali, in one short, planet-shrinking century.

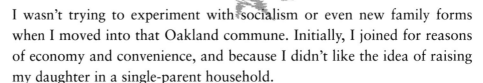

I wasn't trying to experiment with socialism or even new family forms when I moved into that Oakland commune. Initially, I joined for reasons of economy and convenience, and because I didn't like the idea of raising my daughter in a single-parent household.

The commune, known as Harwood House, was located in an old three-story mansion on Harwood Avenue, and was composed of nine members, some of whom eventually left and were replaced by new ones. We were not connected by any spiritual or political agenda, and sometimes we lived like individual apartment-dwellers who just happened to share a kitchen. Other times we became a close-knit community, especially when we rallied around someone going through a crisis, or on nights when we ate together and sang songs as we did the dishes, or celebrated a birthday or holiday.

At various times during my decade there, Harwood House hosted meditation classes, poetry readings, and slide shows, and increasing numbers of people became connected to the commune. Traditions began to form, such as the huge annual Halloween celebration, attended by past and present housemates and their relatives and friends. Harwood House grew from a commune into a community.

Living with so many people taught me how hard it is to walk one's talk about selflessness and universal love. Especially when it's one's turn to do the composting. Life at Harwood House was good exercise for my heart muscle. Also, the success of this group-living experiment renewed my faith in my own political and spiritual principles. I realized that we can indeed live our alternatives.

Still, despite having a fine relationship, and an extended family of friends, I sometimes feel nostalgic for that idealized version of the American family—the one that never did exist in reality. I find myself longing for the fantasy that was projected in advertisements, or in my parents' desires.

Like many, I clashed a lot with my parents in the 1960s. The generation gap was wider than the genetic link; our views and interests were so different that I found it hard to be with them at all. Besides, I had rejected their dreams for me, and I felt guilty about displeasing them. I had even given up on their God. As Ram Dass is fond of saying, "I'm only Jewish on my parents' side."

I tried once to introduce my parents to the other side of my life by teaching them how to meditate. Within minutes of beginning to watch his breath, my father fell asleep and began snoring. My mother immediately burst out laughing and said, "That's what I do every night. Snoring meditation."

Typically, as I got older I came to love and appreciate my parents more and more, and I think they finally began to realize that even though I hadn't quite turned out as they had hoped, I was nonetheless what they called a "good person," and leading a relatively happy life. Whenever I long for those illusory ideals, I try to remind myself of that.

For me and many of my friends, the decade or so after the '60s was a time of compromise, of reconciling our ideals with reality, both personally and politically. We learned that it was not so easy to turn the world around, and that, furthermore, we would have to face the consequences of growing up and making a living. America was no longer a free ride, and we were no longer so young.

Perhaps it was partially because of our disappointments, that during the '70s many baby boomers began to turn the focus of their idealism inward. Even if we couldn't change the culture or stop the arms race, we might be able to change ourselves. Furthermore, many of us had concluded that the only way to really transform the world was to increase consciousness and compassion within each individual. One way or another, we were determined to create a new age.

LET'S HAVE A NEW AGE

Chapter Nine

What the modern cultural environment has required of us is an enormous extroversion of attention and energy for the purpose of reshaping the Earth into a global industrial economy. For two centuries we have been subordinating the planet and our deepest personal needs to that project. This great act of collective alienation lies at the root of both the environmental and individual neurosis. In some way, at some point, a change of direction, a therapeutic turning inward, had to take place within a culture as maniacally driven as ours has been by the need to achieve and conquer.

THEODORE ROSZAK,
THE VOICE OF THE EARTH

133

Over the past few decades, a so-called "new age" has emerged out of the American underground, the bastard child of a beatnik father and a hippie mother, midwifed by renegade Western psychologists and Eastern sages. This multiheaded creature is made up of myths and symbols from every corner of the world, united by the dominant American gene for utopian idealism. Its followers include a few wise people trying to figure out new ways of evolving, some hucksters trying to make a buck, and a whole lot of people looking for a community of shared belief.

I sometimes deny any connection to the new age because I think it sounds pretentious, like saying that you think you are one of the evolved ones, one step ahead of the rest of the culture or the species. But when the Dalai Lama was asked if *he* was part of the new age, he said, "I hope so. I think we should all be happy to have a new age."

In general, I believe the new age can be divided into two basic camps: One is devoted to enhancing the individual self, to building up weak or downtrodden egos; the other is devoted to shrinking the self, to breaking down separate identities and reconnecting people to community, nature, and the great mysteries. These two projects need not be mutually exculsive. As one new age psychologist says, "You have to be somebody before you can be nobody."

New age thinking is perhaps best characterized by the word "wholistic," which has become a cliche, but nonetheless defines a distinct worldview, a scientific premise, and a code of behavior. The wholistic approach is currently permeating all fields of human understanding, creating a kind of psycho-socio-sexual-politico-eco-anthro-spiritual revolution—in many different wholistic combinations.

By the 1970's, when the new age came along, I had already tried the traditional psychotherapies. Freudian analysis had left me hopelessly hung up on my mother and sex—and made me aware of how the two fit together in ways I had never imagined. I went from the Oedipal to the pedestrian when I started seeing a Jungian therapist. That is, I came to realize that I had a fallen archetype, and maybe should be going to a foot doctor instead.

In the late sixties, I began exploring all sorts of transformational techniques: body therapies, gestalt workshops, consciousness-raising seminars, personality assessments, herbal healings, and even health-enhancing home appliances. Even after starting a Buddhist meditation practice, which I believe to be the ultimate healing process, I continued to sample from the new age cornucopia.

I admit, my motives were mixed. Partly, I was still searching for perfect moments, another good high. Since drugs had let us down or proved too costly, many of my friends and I tried spiritual and psychological techniques to get naturally high, or "high on the natch," as we called it. Other times I took part in new age experiments out of sheer curiosity, or just for a good news story. Still, I would not have been disappointed to accidentally find a shortcut to nirvana—a weekend workshop in visualization or a special theraputic tweak of my psyche that would leave me forever at peace.

During my first few years in California, I tried various body therapies, such as polarity and rolfing. The idea behind these techniques was that your tight muscles reflected your neuroses. If you could somehow release the "blockages" in your body, your energy would flow more smoothly and you might become as happy as a jellyfish. A couple of the practitioners who worked on me seemed to be literally tearing my muscles and tendons off my bones and shoving them into new positions in order to get me into "alignment." I suspect that these bodyworkers may be the ones who coined the phrase, "No pain, no gain."

As an American, I am thoroughly conditioned to reject that sentiment, and to believe that the simple act of buying a new consumer item can make me happy. Playing to this belief, all sorts of aids and accoutrements have been invented to serve the Western seeker, products that promise to hasten you toward super health, higher consciousness, nirvana, satori, or wherever it was you thought you wanted to go. The spirit of commerce cannot resist the commerce in spirit.

For several years I had a negative ion generator in my house. Negative ions are supposed to be good for you. They supposedly counteract air pollution, and some claim they even get rid of bad vibes. I remember being somewhat skeptical, but I eventually broke down and bought one at my local health food store. After trying it out for a few weeks, I went back and told the salesperson that the device didn't seem to make any difference in my mood or general health. I'll never forget how he looked me in the eye and said very sincerely, "Maybe you just aren't sensitive enough to notice the difference." I should have let my anger show, but I was into simply labeling and watching emotions at the time, so I reluctantly took my negative ion generator back home and plugged it in again.

After a few years it got tossed into a back closet, where it serves as a periodic reminder of how much I have fallen for in my search for salvation. On the other hand, I will never know whether those negative ions actually worked or not, because there were just too many other variables in the mix. It is possible that I would be very sick or even dead today if that generator hadn't been filling my living space with negative ions throughout the 1970s.

Negative-heel shoes were another new age fad, one that many of us leaned over backward for. I used to do commercials on KSAN for Roots Natural Footwear, a chain of negative-heel shoe stores. (Could this have been part of my rebellion against my father, who mostly sold high heels?) It is hard to believe now, but for a few years back in the 1970s there were entire shoe stores that sold only negative-heel shoes—sandals and hiking boots and even dress shoes. I forget exactly what they were supposed to do for you, but they did slope downward in the heel, giving the wearer a slightly backward slant. Some say they felt "laid back" while wearing them, while others report feeling more like one of the Fabulous Furry Freak Brothers in the famous "truckin' " cartoon—in a kind of perpetual strutting mode.

Of course I fell for the spirulina fad. Spirulina is algae, and for a while the entire new age population was gobbling it up like a pod of hungry whales. You can take spirulina in pill form or as a powder that you mix into shakes and fruit drinks. Eaten straight, it tastes terrible. It must have been the original bitter herb way back before land was created. I forget now what eating algae was supposed to cure or enhance. Maybe it got you in touch with your inner fish. After all, ontogeny recapitulates phylogeny. Another piece of seaweed, Gill?

One of my favorite new age products is a simple massaging device called the "MA-roller," perhaps after a great mother masseuse goddess. You can give yourself a spinal massage and back rub anytime you want by rolling around on your MA-roller. According to the ads, this wondrous wooden massaging wheel was "designed by a student of Chinese acupuncture who is also a student of yoga...and is a result of meditations on the five elements as given in the Huang Ti Nei Jing (The Yellow Emperors's Classic of Internal Medicine)." Mercy! I bought it, I used it, and I loved my MA-roller.

I also once owned a "Footsie Roller," which was kind of a MA-roller for the soles of your feet. The retailers told me that nerve endings in one's feet are connected to all other parts of the body, including internal organs, and massaging those nerve endings might make me happy as a clam.

Several other devices claim to work on the soles of your feet. If you aren't concerned about using electricity you can purchase an "electrically heated foot massage roller." And if you are just plain lazy, I assume you can also achieve the benefits of foot massage by wearing—if you can possibly stand it—those little sandals and slippers with the rubber points sticking up all over the insole. No pain, no gain. Walk on, oh seeker, walk on!

Speaking of pain, a few entrepreneurs have profited from Westerners who found themselves sitting uncomfortably in meditation. Few of us seem to be genetically programmed for legs that move easily into the preferred Asian posture, that cross-legged, thigh-locked, reverse twist of legs and feet known as the lotus position. Some Eastern yogis say the lotus encloses the body's energy in a special way that enhances meditation. For this reason, and also because it looks stylish and cool, many Westerners have gone through agonizing efforts to remain seated on the floor in some facimile of the lotus pose while meditating. Thankfully, the new age marketplace has come to our aid with benches, back rests, bolsters, knee pillows, straps, and even elaborate balloon-like chairs—all designed to keep you from suffering while you contemplate the Buddha's first Noble Truth: the inevitablity of suffering.

Many new age seekers have been fascinated with pyramids. I remember visiting a famous California retreat center in the mid '70s and seeing a group of people walking around completely naked except for tiny pyramid-shaped hats on their heads. They claimed to be experiencing "pyramid power." I myself have never felt anything special either inside or outside of a pyramid, and I wonder if their reputation is based solely on the fact that they preserved Egyptian mummies for so long. Or maybe I am so skeptical that I will only feel pyramid power if I sit down on the sharply pointed top of one.

Of course, if I believe that the material and spiritual are One, how can I deny that there are many ways into the mystic. Even stones may be of use. I once saw an advertisement for a "lapis meditation head band" which was supposed to "open your mystical third eye." You might also try an Indian stone pyramid necklace, to give you "strong, strong vibrations." Another advertisement claimed that lapis combined with silver and worn in the belly button builds up the energy of your "will chakra." (In fact, there are special stones and colors to help you develop or "open" each of your body's seven chakras, or energy centers.) In face of all this, I think I would be happy if I could open up my "will-not" chakra, but nobody seems to know where it's located.

Maybe I'm not enlightened yet because I just haven't hit the right combination of workshops or products. Reading through new age magazines I see that I could still have my biorhythms read, buy a biofeedback machine to monitor my alpha waves, an isolation tank to create a perfect environment for meditation, some full-spectrum lighting to enhance my "light-chemical mood balance," or the "Natural Rhythm Futon" which is not, as the name seems to imply, a birth-control bed, but a way to achieve some kind of moving bodily harmony with one's mattress while sleeping. I could also try the "Dream Pillow," which is stuffed with hops. The people who sell dream pillows cite "herbal literature documents" to conclude that hops—not in your brew, but under your head—can promote restful sleep and pleasant colorful dreams.

Over the years I have seen a few poetic come-ons that maybe I should have pursued, like the one that read, "Getting rid of what you haven't got! A one dollar book on Mantra, Inner Self, Value of Dying, Guru, Flying, Paradise. Enclose one dollar and write to OM, 113 Friar Way, Campbell, California." Another offered a slightly different, but equally vague, range of eclectic pursuits: "We excell in matters of holistic health, biomagnetism, earthradiation exposures, ESP, the Unexplained. Only $13.50."

My confused search for both kicks and consciousness is probably best revealed by my fascination with tantric sex, which continued long after my return from India. Intrigued by the possibility of achieving higher consciousness and better orgasms at the same time, in 1975 I attended an introductory lecture by a group in Berkeley who combined tantric sex and rebirthing into a program called "Sexual Enlightenment Workshops." Those who decided to enroll in the workshop were promised a "sex karma cleansing." I didn't sign up. The process sounded to me like it could hurt a lot, depending on which part of my sex karma got put through the ringer.

Later, a girlfriend and I actually did end up taking a tantric sexuality workshop in Berkeley. The class turned out to be good for a little voyeurism, and perhaps we did end up experiencing slightly prolonged orgasms, but consciousness was definitely not the main thing being raised.

For a while afterward, we tried to practice the most common tantric sexual position, which has the man seated and the woman in his lap facing him. This posture is called the "yab-yum," yab referring to male energy and yum to female. Probably the most enduring thing to come out of my tantric sexual experiences is this blues-shuffle song I wrote, called the "Tantric Boogie":

> *I'll be your yab*
> *You be my yum.*
> *Put your legs around me 'til we're sittin' tum to tum.*
> *The Eastern ways can be divine*
> *So line your chakras up with mine,*
> *And let's do the yab-yum baby 'til the cows come home.*
>
> *You be my yin*
> *I'll be your yang.*
> *We can do the Eastern thing with a little Western twang.*

Everything is everything, it's been said
So as long as we fell out of bed
Let's do the yab-yum baby, 'til the cows come home.

Come over here, sit on my lap, and let yourself go.
The gurus who are in the know say
It's much better if you do it...do it...do it...slow...

So, I'll be your yang
You be my yin.
Let's breathe along together
Out in, out in, out in, out in (faster)...
Someday we will all be one,
And getting there is half the fun
So let's do the yab-yum baby, 'till the cows come home.
Yuuummmm....

Word must have traveled through the Asian guru grapevine that the United States was hungry for Eastern mysticism, because by the mid '70s a veritable gaggle of gurus had descended on California from the Far East. Every week you would see posters advertising the arrival of another Indian swami or Tibetan lama or Korean Zen master. And for every guru there were plenty of gurupies, refugees from harsh Jehovah and middle-class materialism looking for a kinder, gentler spiritual home. Many were quite willing to hand over their lives to any man in a turban or robe who smiled at them like daddy never had. Of course we went for it. And why not? Our society was a battleground of competition and jealousy; people were starving to hear that they were wonderful, radiant beings of light and that everything is perfect in the cosmic overview. And it is, isn't it?

As special features producer at KSAN, I had the perfect entree into any spiritual scene that interested me, and could interview all the hottest gurus who came to town. During one on-air interview, Swami Muktananda bopped me on the head with a peacock feather as a blessing, supposedly transferring his shakti-pat (divine energy) directly into me. I actually went blank for a minute or so, which meant that the listeners heard only silence, and my producer became very agitated about the radio sin known as "dead air." When I came around, I asked Muktananda to perform a miracle that everyone could experience. He replied, "Just look at the workings of your own mind and body. That should be miracle enough for anyone."

Tibetan master Chogyam Trungpa Rinpoche stayed totally lucid while drinking an entire bottle of saki during our hour-long interview. He told me that the Chinese invasion of Tibet was a kind of collective karma, a result of the corruption of Tibetan Buddhist monastic institutions. A renegade, and self-proclaimed "crazy wisdom" master, Trungpa was one of the best translators of Eastern wisdom to the West. He founded the Naropa Institute in Boulder, Colorado, and eventually attracted a huge following of artists and intellectuals, including Allen Ginsberg and Phillip Glass.

I also followed the careers of some enterprising Westerners who decided that they, too, were spiritual masters. Many of these self-proclaimed teachers mixed together a few nuggets of Eastern wisdom, a little psychodrama, some techniques from the Catholic confessional, and a dollop of Jewish chutzpah or Irish blarney to create their own unique paths to enlightenment. Some of them had real wisdom to offer, but there were several very suspicious characters, to say the least.

In 1976 I interviewed one Dr. Fredrick Lenz. At the time, Dr. Lenz was the Director of Eastern Studies at the New School for Social Research in New York, and had written a book entitled *Lifetimes: True Accounts of Reincarnation*. The book was a fascinating work of sociology, containing well-documented stories of people who recalled past lives, and I found Dr. Lenz to be a lively talk-show guest.

I did not hear of him again until sometime in 1982, when I picked up a new age magazine and saw his picture featured in an advertisement.

Dr. Lenz, who was now calling himself "Atmananda," was promoting himself as some kind of guru. I smiled to myself and tried to imagine his career switch from university professor to cosmic wisdom master. Then in 1983 I began to see full-page color advertisements featuring a much bigger photo of Dr. Lenz, who had since let his curly hair grow out and was now wearing an Indian-style collarless shirt. The picture was taken with back-lighting to give his face a glowing halo effect, and he seemed to be gazing out at the world with love.

Dr. Lenz had also changed his name again, and was now calling himself "Rama, the last incarnation of Vishnu." That's a pretty heavy claim to make, considering that Vishnu is one of the three principle Hindu deities, the one in charge of preserving the world. The Buddha himself is considered one of Vishnu's incarnations. Meanwhile, the text of the advertisement revealed one of the most audacious self-promotions in this or any other new age. In this ad, Dr. Fredrick Lenz, aka Rama, listed his *past life resume*, an irrefutable list of spiritual credentials.

> 1531–1575 *Zen Master, Kyoto, Japan*
> 1602–1671 *Head of Zen Order, Kyoto, Japan*
> 1725–1804 *Master of Monastery, Tibet*
> 1834–1905 *Jnana Yoga Master, India*
> 1912–1945 *Tibetan Lama, Head of Monastic Order, Tibet*
> 1950– *Self Realized Spiritual Teacher*

I don't know whether I believe in reincarnation or not. If it's true, then once you've seen one Dalai Lama, you've seen them all. However, if incarnation does happen, then maybe we should all take out Next Life Insurance.

> *We seem to believe we can be reborn without ever dying. Such is the spiritual version of the American Dream.*
>
> ROLLO MAY, *THE CRY FOR MYTH*

During the '70s and '80s, many esoteric disciplines emerged, seemingly from nowhere, to stake their claim to ultimate reality, and to market pieces of it. Out of curiosity and for a possible news story, I decided to join up with one of these new spiritual groups for a while. Through an ad in a new age magazine, I was led to the San Jose Marriot Hotel for a weekend seminar on "Eckankar," billed as "The Ancient Science of Soul Travel." The people who greeted me in the Marriot convention room told me that Eckankar is the method that all the great saints have used to find the secret kingdom of God while still in their physical bodies. I learned that Socrates, Plato, Jesus, and Moses had all practiced soul travel as students of Eckankar, the oldest spiritual wisdom in the world.

The meaning of Eckankar is supposedly revealed to certain enlightened masters throughout the ages, and in our time it has made itself known to three Americans: first to Paul Twitchell, who wrote scores of books on the subject, then to an engineer from Ohio named Darwin Gross, and then to Harold Klemp. It seems odd, but is perhaps quite appropriate for our age, that all of these "living ECK Masters" look like corporate middle-managers. When it comes to soul travel, these folks are apparently traveling business class.

When I left the Marriot, I was given a book entitled *Eckankar: The Key to Secret Worlds*, by Sri Paul Twitchell, which was full of exercises for would-be soul travelers. I tried a couple of them for a few weeks. One, for example, tells you to lie on your back, place a colored disk on your forehead between your eyebrows, and then stare at it for at least five minutes without blinking. The instructions tell you to increase the time spent staring at your disk by another minute every night until eventually you are absorbed into the disk and your ordinary environment fades away. Then, according to the book, an altogether different type of landscape will take its place, "usually with someone like the living ECK Master appearing to give an explanation of where you are and what is happening." I would have loved to meet the living ECK Master in a kind of cosmic virtual reality, but I could never figure out how to actually see my colored disk when it was on my forehead. For soul travel, I went back to Aretha Franklin.

My desire for some great revelation that would awaken humanity or transform the world has led me into some questionable enthusiasms. For instance, in the spring of 1973, astronomers sighted a comet they named Kohoutec; they predicted "a momentous astronomical event" when the comet passed near the earth. New age seekers adopted Kohoutec as their own, holding rituals to welcome the comet as harbinger of the Age of Aquarius. I helped pump up the energy for Kohoutec on my radio broadcasts. The comet, however, fizzled out. It was barely visible, even to astronomers.

Undaunted, new agers gathered again in 1986, this time for a planetary happening that coincided with an ancient Mayan prophecy. The event was dubbed the "Harmonic Convergence." I tried to negotiate with the program director of my radio station for time to talk about the event on the air, but he would only let me chant "om" for thirty seconds. The "convergence" might have had some effect on the planet's future, or added a necessary grace note to the music of the spheres. After all, not too much later the Berlin Wall came down, nuclear disarmament began, and Rabin and Arafat shook hands. These events were nearly unimaginable before the Harmonic Convergence and, given all the variables, how can we ever know that it *didn't* herald a new era?

A decade earlier, the 1976 World Symposium on Humanity had tried to create cosmic consciousness through satellite television. Promoted like an entertainment spectacular, the World Symposium was held simultaneously in Toronto, London, and Los Angeles, and featured Buckminster Fuller, Ralph Nader, Marshall McLuhan, Ram Dass, Dick Gregory, Joseph Campbell, Carl Rogers, Laura Huxley, and Fritjof Capra. I tried to get my radio station to let me cover the event, but the management concluded that there just wasn't enough rock and roll in the program.

In the late 1970s and early 1980s, I began noticing that the most popular teachers on the new age circuit were ethereal beings. These disembodied entities were "channeled" to new age audiences by people who claimed to be "mediums." All at once, it seemed, a multitude of spirit entities had decided to make themselves accessible. Some came from the traditional heavens, many from Atlantis, some from inside the earth itself—and all of them seemed to have important things to say to the people of our planet at this moment in history. If I may be so bold as to summarize, most spirit guides said—and still say—something like, "The apocalypse is coming, but it's going to be all right because you are all wonderful beings, and eternal to boot. So don't worry. Love each other and be happy." Not a bad message at all.

Seekers may have been drawn to spirit guides after so many of the gurus *with* bodies turned out to be charlatans. Of course, you do still have to go through a medium and risk interference. After all, as Marshall McLuhan said, the medium is the message.

I attended a few Bay Area "psychic fairs" to see if I could get acquainted with some of these entities. At one such gathering, I found a series of perhaps thirty booths set up around a large conference room. Each booth featured a single female medium (not one male) seated at a table with some amulet before her—usually a crystal, a feather, a burning candle, or some incense. Some of these mediums looked to me like circus fortune-tellers who had psychically discovered where the real money was now to be made. Several other women in the room had a sweet, spacy, love-the-world vibe, like Deadheads who had taken their acid visions seriously. A few seemed to be former suburban housewives who had been visited by the spirit of Mr. Clean once too often, and now wanted to be in a trance that was completely different from housework.

I talked to several of the mediums at length. One buxom woman with thick lipstick and a pile of permed curls said she was channeling "a healing guide named Master Kirk." She told me that her Master Kirk had nothing to do with Star Trek. Her Master Kirk would simply come down and put his hands on her shoulders and then guide her healing sessions.

Another woman told me she was channeling "the White Brotherhood," which was the collective energy of master teachers, including Christ, Mohammed, Buddha, Zoroaster, etc. A few mediums were channeling women spirits, and one in particular said she could transfer the energy of Joan of Arc to any female who came to see her regularly.

One thing that interests me is that mediums don't have to take direct responsiblity for their predictions or healing; they can always blame the spirits. More than once I have been told by a psychic or medium that they were "having trouble getting through," or that there was some "interference," or that their spirit guide did not feel like talking today. Of course, the spirits may have just decided not to pick up when they heard that I was calling.

For a while, the most famous medium was J.Z. Knight, a Tacoma, Washington housewife who went to beauty school and then to business college, and finally found her calling. One day, Knight claims she was just standing in her kitchen when suddenly an apparition named Ramtha appeared, saying he was a thirty-five-thousand-year-old warrior from the lost continent of Atlantis. Ramtha also told J.Z. Knight that she was his daughter, and soon thereafter she began channeling her alleged father in a gravely voice, which eventually attracted the likes of Shirley MacLaine and Linda Evans. Those who believe call each other "Ramsters" and have paid up to $1,000 to be in an audience where Ramtha speaks. J.Z. Knight is now worth millions of dollars and reportedly living in luxury on a fifty-acre ranch. Several times I tried to interview Ms. Knight, but I was always put off by her secretary, the medium's medium.

Another former housewife achieved notoriety in a different spiritual circle after she attracted Ram Dass as her disciple. Joya (Green) Santanya, a Jewish Brooklyn housewife in her late thirties with three kids, one day got into her bathtub and started doing breathing exercises in order to lose weight. She reports that suddenly she went into trance and was visited by none other than Ram Dass's guru, Neem Karoli Maharaj-ji (deceased by that time), who sat down right next to the tub and began talking. The story delighted the spiritual underground as one of those cosmic/comic twists of fate. Jewish uncle Ram Dass would of course find his new guru in the form of a Jewish housewife from Brooklyn! It was perfect.

The channeling craze spread to even the most respectable new age venues. At Esalen Institute in 1979, a woman on staff named Jenny O'Connor began to channel "the Nine," whom she described as a group of eight-million-year-old mass-energy entities from the star Sirius. At one point the Esalen staff were consulting with the Nine for advice on how to run the Institute.

Despite the hype and confusion, I try to stay open to channeling and, in fact, I am now actively seeking to become a medium for Harpo Marx. So far he hasn't said anything to me or through me, but his air-horn has woken me up at night several times already.

> *Be here now! (Pause) Whoops, you missed it! But don't worry, the here and now will be presented again soon, so stay alert!*
>
> THE SWAMI FROM MIAMI

During these millenium-ending, paradigm-shifting times, there is a lot of room for creativity. In a new age everybody gets to fashion his or her own religion, mixing and matching pieces of various traditions. There is a danger to this, of course, especially if people only pick the easy stuff.

Sometimes the spiritual mixtures can be confusing as well. I once interviewed a woman at a Christian rally who was wearing a jacket embroidered: "Shiksas for Jews for Jesus." When I asked her how she came up with that slogan, she explained, "Well, it's true. I am a shiksa, and I am also a member of Jews for Jesus. So my jacket says, 'Shiksas for Jews for Jesus.' Is that so strange?"

When cultures collide, mixed metaphors abound and humor naturally arises. The meetings of East and West have provided some especially good comic possibilities. In my travels through Asia, for instance, I couldn't help but notice how so many of the young Western spiritual seekers were

GO OUT AND MAKE SOME OF YOUR OWN

Jewish. This became even more apparent back in America, where the four founding teachers of the Buddhist Insight Meditation Society in Massachusetts turned out to be Goldstein, Kornfield, Schwartz, and Salzberg. It sounds more like a law firm than a Buddhist teaching group. While some people speculated about the reason why so many Jews were drawn to Buddhism, I decided to take advantage of it.

The inspiration came to me at a meditation retreat. Bored with watching breath after breath, my mind started working on an idea that would bring Jew and Buddhist together in a great East-West spritual synthesis. Other people had started cults and religions, so why not me? As long as there's no marytrdom involved, the religion racket seems like a fine way to earn a living.

What came to me was a synthesis—a spiritual philosophy that combined the strengths of both Jews and Buddhists. I began to realize that they are a perfect complement to each other. Why not unite the wordless wisdom of the Buddhists with Jewish verbal skills, enhancing both in the process? Why not fuse the cool detachment of the Buddhist with schmaltzy Jewish sentiment, creating a full-spectrum emotional approach to life? Out of this blend of two great cultural and spiritual traditions would come the Buish people (not to be confused with the Jews for Krishna, also known as "Hind-jews"). Being basically Westerners, the Buish people would no longer have to walk the Buddha's traditional "middle path." Instead, they could take the upper-middle path.

One day in my meditation fantasy, the Buish guru made himself known to me. His name is "the Swami from Miami," and he is a fairly wise Indian fortune-teller and/or fortune-seeker who decided to relocate from India to Miami Beach, where he ends up reading palms and astrological charts for old Jewish ladies on the boardwalk. At night he performs Indian rope tricks in the lobby of the Fontainbleu Hotel.

Throughout my meditation retreat, the Swami kept appearing to share his teachings with me. He told me that he knows some shortcuts to enlightenment. One has to do with the Zen koan, which is an unsolvable riddle employed to frustrate the rational mind. The Swami figured that if he could combine a few of these koans, he could create even more frustration and therefore achieve quicker realization in his students. So he took three of the most popular Zen koans: "What is the sound of one hand clapping?", "Does a dog have Buddha nature?", and "If everything returns to the One, to what does the One return?" The Swami fused these into one super-koan: "What is the sound of one dog returning to the One?" Barking is not the answer.

The Swami also apparently tried to convince his disciples that the quickest way to discover your true inner-self is to peek in through your anus. This, of course, requires the ability to bring your head down through your legs and upward a bit, which in turn requires some very advanced yoga skills. In fact, after all the yoga required, it isn't much of a shortcut after all. The few who were able to accomplish this feat of becoming a human pretzel report only that their inner-nature is a bit smelly. But again, as the great sages say, "Self-knowledge is usually bad news."

The Swami told me that many of his disciples left him after he came up with a rather bizarre "spiritual shortcut." One day he jumped up from meditating and exclaimed to the students sitting in the room with him, "If it is true that you are what you eat, then why be a vegetable?" His students looked at him, and after a minute had to nod in agreement. Then the Swami smiled and said, "If you are what you eat, then perhaps you should eat people who are smarter and more spiritually advanced than you are!"

After the retreat, I told my comic friend Darryl Henriques about the Swami from Miami, and he immediately went into trance and became a West Coast medium for the Swami. Recently Darryl told me that the Swami from Miami has refined both his dialectical and dietary doctrines. Instead of saying "You are what you eat," the Swami now tells his disciples that it is more accurate to say, "You are what you don't poop."

Aside from promoting the Buish doctrine, I am helping to make other changes vital to the sucessful transmission of Eastern wisdom to the West. For example, in Asia there are two main branches of Buddhism, each of which are called "yana" or vehicle. There's the Hinayana, which translates literally as "the lesser vehicle," and the Mahayana, which translates as "the greater vehicle." We need an altogether different vehicle for American Buddhists, and I think it should be the "Hahayana," or "funny vehicle." If you wish to visualize this mode of transportation along the path to enlightenment, try to imagine the Buddha riding in an Edsel.

The Hahayana teachings are transmitted primarily through the use of knock-knock jokes. A disciple will come to visit the guru and say, "Knock, knock." The guru then poses the fundamental question of all great wisdom traditions, "Who's there?"

The Hahayana cannon is still being written but so far it consists of three main texts, *The Sioux City Sutra*, *The Double-Breasted Sutra*, and *How Does That Sutra*. These texts imply that the human condition is some kind of joke, and the whole point of the practice, as well as the point of your entire life, is to "get it." If you don't get it, you'll have to be reborn and listen to the same joke over and over again, until you finally do.

> *Since everything is but an apparition, perfect in being what it is, having nothing to do with good or bad, acceptance or rejection, one may well burst out in laughter.*
>
> LONG CHEN PA, TIBETAN MEDITATION MASTER

I often wonder why I have been so attracted to new age phenomena. Am I newly self-aware, or merely self-absorbed? Maybe it's just human nature to desire something you don't have. I had plenty of social and political freedom, and therefore was able to chase after absolute freedom. I, and many of my generation, began seeking relief, not only from our specific human conditioning, but from the human condition itself.

Rather than "new age," however, I think maybe we should call this era the new "middle ages," after the time between the fall of the Roman

Empire and the Renaissance. The parallels are striking. The old order is rapidly fading, and the shape of what's coming is not yet clear.

Personally, I feel as though I'm stuck between two paradigms and a hard place, doing the mythological splits. I've got one foot in the old country and another on the astral plane. During my meanderings through various workshops and retreats, I often feel suspended between stories that are too old to have meaning for me and those that are too new to have gained any. I go to rituals and sometimes catch myself thinking how odd that I am doing this—at a sweatlodge chanting an old Native American song, just syllables to me, "Haya Ho-ya Ho-ya Ho-ya..." or going up to an altar to have my head patted by some Tibetan lama in a blessing that is guaranteed to shorten the number of rebirths I will have. Suddenly, I find myself asking, "What in the Judeo-Christian Heaven's name am I doing here?" Often I have no good answer.

While I can't always enter these ceremonies with full spirit, I usually manage to find some metaphoric meaning in them. I also honor the attempt to revive the art of ritual. A sense of religious awe and humility is generally missing in our high-speed urban lives, and we are hungry for new ways to understand ourselves, as well as both grieve and celebrate that understanding. With the loss of our traditional beliefs and rituals, many of us also lost our sense of community. Much of the new age is an attempt to find a new community of shared belief and to create ritual events that will speak to and unite that community.

This issue was clarified for me in 1992, when I was asked to teach Buddhist meditation at a gathering of environmental activists. The retreat was attended by African-American Southern Baptists, Latino Catholic farmworkers, Native American tribal leaders, and a group of Caucasian baby-boomers with their grab-bag of Asian and new age practices, all linked by their involvement in various environmental campaigns. The organizers wanted these people to leave their political work behind for a week, and gather just to share the spiritual traditions that give them sustenance.

On the first day of the retreat, I was somewhat dismayed when only white people showed up at my meditation class. I began to understand the reason later that evening when Starhawk, a leader of the neo-pagan, Wicca movement from California, was scheduled to lead a moon-worshiping ritual. Outside the dining hall the Southern Baptists were talking together, and I overheard one woman say, "I ain't goin' out to howl at the moon with some witch!" Needless to say, neither the Catholic farmworkers, nor the Native Americans showed up at Starhawk's ceremony either. These people felt no need to seek other ways to connect with the mysteries or their own spirituality. In fact, they found some of our new age practices rather bizarre, and in some cases, even blasphemous. The white, middle-class boomers, on the other hand, were not grounded in any tradition, and therefore were open to everything. We joined in the Native American blessings, nodded in agreement with the fiery words of the Baptist preacher talking about Jesus-as-revolutionary, and then went to sit in our adopted form of silent meditation, closing with the traditional Buddhist blessing, "may all beings be liberated."

Awe is the salve
that will heal our eyes.

RUMI, *DELICIOUS LAUGHTER*

Within the new age ethos is an important emphasis on celebration and the ideal of living in the moment. Many of the workshops and retreats I have attended encourage people to rejoice in the experience of life. In some sense, emphasizing the moment is a rejection of materialism, saying that we already have what we need. It's the same lesson I learned in meditation.

Meanwhile, the imported religious practices from Asia and the neo-pagan movements are shaking Judeo-Christian culture, calling it to re-evaluate itself. There are many gods and goddesses finding a new home in

America today (they come from the colonies), and just as biodiversity is important to the survival of life, so too perhaps is "deo-diversity." To find a way out of our current dilemmas we will need help from all the gods we can find.

Finally, I think the new age is responding to the perennial call for renewal of metaphor, for rebirth of the true religious spirit of universal love and wonder, heard urgently in this century again, and spoken most eloquently in the words of D. H. Lawrence:

> *Man has little needs and deeper needs. We have fallen into the mistake of living from our little needs till we have almost lost our deeper needs in a sort of madness....Let us prepare now for the death of our present 'little' life, and the re-emergence in a bigger life, in touch with the moving cosmos.*
>
> *It is a question, practically of relationship. We must get back into relation, vivid and nourishing relation to the cosmos and the universe. The way is through daily ritual, and the reawakening. We must once more practise the ritual of dawn and noon and sunset, the ritual of the kindling fire and pouring water, the ritual of the first breath, and the last. This is an affair of the individual and the household, a ritual of day. The ritual of the moon in her phases, of the morning star and the evening star is for men and women separate. Then the ritual of the seasons, with the Drama and the Passion of the soul embodied in procession and dance, this is for the community, an act of men and women, a whole community, in togetherness. And the ritual of the great events in the year of stars is for nations and whole peoples. To these rituals we must return: or we must evolve them to suit our needs. For the truth is, we are perishing for lack of fulfillment of our*

greater needs, we are cut off from the great sources of our inward nourishment and renewal, sources which flow eternally in the universe. Vitally, the human race is dying. It is like a great uprooted tree, with its roots in the air. We must plant ourselves again in the universe.

A PROPOS OF LADY CHATTERLEY'S LOVER

THE LAST NEWS SHOW

The following program has not been approved by U.S. military censors, the Vatican, the Ayatollah, the Kremlin, the FBI, or the FDIC. This program does, however, meet the minimum requirements of the Clean Air Act, even though it does not agree with them.

ONE OF MY KFOG–FM NEWS INTRODUCTIONS, 1984

Although the new age and environmental movement took root in America in the '70s, they almost got blown away by the conservative storm of the Reagan years. Indeed, religious fundamentalism and reactionary politics seemed to sweep across the planet during the 1980s, probably in response to the liberal extremes of the previous decades. Maybe just the yin–yang, doin' it's thang.

In the early 1980s, I was fairly discouraged most of the time. Although meditation helped me maintain some balance, I felt a constant tension and gloom over a world that seemed to have gone mad for money and power. Mammon ruled the '80s, and War was his charioteer. And as far as I could tell, we had at least two evil empires in the world.

I had lost my job at KSAN-FM in 1979, after the station switched formats from rock and roll to what is known as "urban country." They sure 'nuff didn't want any unrepentant hippie doing news commentary for their new target audience, which someone once described as "white-collar rednecks."

But if urban-country music was a contradiction in terms, then so was "classic rock," the offical format of KFOG-FM, where I began working in 1983. I was hired as news director and morning news commentator opposite a disc jockey who called himself "Dung." Regardless of his nom de plume, Dung was a very sweet guy, who was actually quite shy when he wasn't broadcasting. When the microphone was turned on, however, he would switch into his own Wolf Man Jack-like persona, and shout "O-Day!" and "O-Dow!" to express his enthusiasm for his favorite rock music.

I would get up every morning at 5 A.M. and within an hour be wearing my headphones, listening to rock music interspersed with Dung's wild shouts, monitoring the UPI teletype machines and writing newscasts. This was not what my Shiva Baba in India had in mind when he told me to get up before the sun. I challenge even the great Zen masters to keep their Buddha-nature cool under those conditions.

KFOG's classic rock format was aimed at the ageing baby boomers, programming rock and roll hits they grew up with from the 50's onward. "Rem-mem-mem...re-mem-me-mem-ber...." I was hired as a token conscience.

KFOG was a relatively pale version of KSAN and the underground radio of 1969, and it was a long way from being freeform. The self-proclaimed "hippest station in the nation" had research departments and playlists, so that the DJ's creativity was kept to a few choice words (fifteen to twenty seconds) between songs and commercials. Freeform FM radio had turned into little more than a top forty format for the flower children who had, for the most part, joined the economic rat race of the Reagan years. "T-t-t-talkin' 'bout my generation."

Shortly after I started working at KFOG, I got a memo that epitomized the changes that had taken place in FM rock radio, and in the national zeitgeist as well:

> *4/5/83*
>
> *I think we should watch the tendancy to sound too much like we're doing news in 1969. By this, I mean the tendancy to inject more politicism than truly exists in today's environment. I'm speaking specifically about some of your comments on El Salvador and Southeast Asia this morning. The people who carved the political woodwork of the era gone by are now driving BMW's and making a shitload of money for some computer-oriented business. And while they maintain a casual interest in past political climates, their heads are fully committed to the 80's and the new awareness that guides their beliefs. It is a high tech society that we are heading toward and it's extremely important that we are there to accompany this new psychographic with complementary programming, both musically and informationally.*
>
> *The Grateful Dead Special we just ran was sponsored by the U.S. Army. Jerry Rubin is a broker on Wall Street and Jane Fonda is a born-again capitalist. This station's information profile must reflect this, both in style and substance.*
>
> *Let's spend some time discussing this soon. Aside from this point, the only area where you should try to focus yourself better is on the TRAFFIC Reports at the bottom of the hour.*

I must say, my program director knew what he was doing. He understood that the audience for rock and roll had grown into mortgages and families. People had lost interest in radical politics and mysticism, or just didn't have time for them. His programming philosophy was to give aging boomers the musical hits that recalled their past glories, and to keep reminding them of their ultimate hipness. And now for these commercial announcements...

> *What I want to see above all is that this country*
> *remains a country where someone can always get*
> *rich.*
>
> RONALD REAGAN, 1983

In the Orwellian year of 1984, Ronald Reagan was elected for a second term as president: Big Actor was chosen to play Big Brother, and America got carefully scripted doublespeak. The top prize for doublespeak should probably go to the trickle-down theory of economics itself, which says, "Give to the rich to help the poor." Another award goes, of course, to the Peacekeeper Missile.

After his reelection, Reagan asked for a 22 percent increase in U.S. defense spending, starting a major escalation of the nuclear arms race. Only a few months before the election, unaware that his microphone was turned on, Reagan had joked, "My fellow Americans, I'm pleased to tell you today that we've signed legislation that will outlaw Russia forever. We begin bombing in five minutes." Soon after that gaff, the Union of Concerned Scientists decided to set the "doomsday clock" forward to three minutes to midnight. The countdown to Armageddon became the subtext of the Reagan era credo, "get it while you can."

The nuclear arms race was the most absurd competition ever instigated by humans, a macho display of terminal tumescence on the part of two superpowers, fit only for historical pornography. My generation was born alongside the bomb at Hiroshima; we grew up in the 1950s fallout shelters with the nuclear-secrets paranoia of McCarthyism; we came of age with the Cuban missile crisis, and grew into maturity during the menace and mendacity of the '70s and '80s, with ABMs and ICBMs, the Trident, MX, Minuteman, and Pershing IIs, and the SALT talks and START talks; finally, we watched the whole mess come into its dotage with the Reagan Star Wars plan of the late '80s.

The peace movement that remained after Vietnam had turned its focus on nuclear weapons proliferation, and in the late '70s, came up with a great hook, "the nuclear freeze." The idea gained so much popularity that even the politicians had to pay attention. Finally, on May, 4, 1983, the U.S. House of Representatives voted in favor of a nuclear weapons freeze. Three weeks later, the very same members of Congress voted money for basing and flight testing of the MX missile, a weapon that could not be defended against, and one that would start another round of nuclear weapons buildup. The freeze melted into mush in the hot air of Washington, D.C.

The politicians and generals who ran the arms race seemed to be completely blind to its long term impact on the economy or the environment. They were even prepared to destroy part of the earth's atmosphere to make the world safe for their respective ideologies. Until the technology was outlawed by a United Nations treaty on biological and environmental warfare, both the United States and the Soviet Union were designing laser weapons that would burn holes in the ozone layer right over enemy territory. They hoped that the sun's ultraviolet radiation could be targeted on crops or military installations, or maybe even an entire damn country. Hell, fry 'em to a crisp if you have to!

This military plan to tamper with nature was outrageous, but an even better example of Cold War madness was the proposal to alter the earth's orbit. Although the idea apparently did not receive much serious consideration, some Pentagon strategists once suggested that a significant number of powerful Atlas booster rockets be set up in a field in the Midwest somewhere. The idea was that if the Soviet Union launched a first strike, then all the rockets could be fired off simultaneously, using the accumulated thrust to change the speed or direction of our planet's orbit. If the earth slowed down or tilted a bit, then the incoming Soviet missiles would lose their accuracy and miss their intended targets in the United States. I don't know what code name was given to this Pentagon proposal, but I called it "The Orbit-uary."

Star Wars was not that much farther fetched. This military scheme was, in fact, part of U.S. military strategy long before Reagan became president. Way back in the Eisenhower administration, the Pentagon was already making plans to install U.S. nuclear weapons on the moon. The generals figured that the Soviets would then have to launch a strike against our moon missiles at least two days before they could attack the United States itself. If they didn't attack our moon missiles first, we would be able to retaliate and blow them up as well—two days later. This idea was part of the Cold War strategy known as Mutual Assured Destruction, or MAD. No wonder Alfred E. Neuman keeps grinning.

Finally, the nuclear arms race came to an end with the collapse of the Soviet empire. It was true that the United States had won, but only by making the Soviet Union spend a larger percentage of their gross national product on unusable weapons systems. Both sides will be paying for generations to come.

One major problem now is figuring out what to do with the huge nuclear arsenals. After the Soviet Union's demise, some experts decided that we could reduce the threat of accidental firings by retargeting all the missiles out to sea. One U.S. general told a congressional committee, "That way, if there is an accident, the bombs will only kill a few whales."

I could find no greater post–Cold War irony than when the Bush administration agreed to buy 500 metric tons of bomb-grade uranium from dismantled Russian nuclear warheads. The Department of Energy said they would use that uranium to fuel nuclear power plants in the United States. The Soviet warheads would reach American targets at last! Nobody, it seemed, remembered the Trojan Horse.

In order to justify continuing budgets of hundreds of billions of dollars, the Pentagon has decided it now needs to develop the ability to fight two wars simultaneously, the "win-win" strategy. For this purpose, the weapons labs are working on smaller sized nuclear bombs, known as mini-nukes.

According to news reports, the Pentagon has also put more focus on nonlethal weapons, quite a switch from the neutron bomb, which kills people but leaves buildings intact. One such weapon emits low-frequency sound waves which cause enemy troops to double over and vomit or defecate uncontrollably. What a great idea! We could have wars where nobody gets hurt, just humiliated. "Look, the enemy is pooping in their uniforms!" Another nonlethal weapon in the works is a chemical which creates such a slippery surface that troops fall down and tanks are unable to manuever. This is Keystone Cops warfare and I'm all for it. But the best weapon of all would be a potent dose of nitrous oxide—get them laughing and they're yours.

The only problem with nonlethal weapons is overpopulation. Approximately 100 million people were killed in this century's wars. Without lethal combat we might have to think of some other way to thin out the human herds.

Throughout the Reagan years, the political left in the Bay Area was deeply committed to the Sandinista cause in Nicaragua. Many of us saw the Sandinistas as heroes, not so different from ourselves really, an idealistic group of young people committed to social justice and new human values. Their revolution, however—more urgent and real—had actually succeeded. They overthrew the arrogant and despised dictator, Anastasio Somoza, whose family had claimed ownership of over 50 percent of all the land in Nicaragua, and who had held power through military terror and the generous support of the United States government.

In 1979, a month after the Sandinista revolution, I went to Nicaragua to help some friends make a film about Father Ernesto Cardenal, who had been named the new government's Minister of Culture. Cardenal was a world-famous poet and had spent several years in the United States as a Trappist novice studying under noted religious scholar Thomas Merton. During the filming, I remember Cardenal telling us, "To be a good Christian in Central America today, one must serve the poor, and that means becoming a revolutionary." Like Father Cardenal, many of the Sandinistas were devout Christians. But Uncle Sam could only see Red, and that meant *godless* communism.

The United States imposed an economic blockade against Nicaragua, destroying any chance for the Sandinista experiment to succeed. Most appalling was that the Reagan administration stooped so low as to support the Contra rebels, known drug smugglers and murderers. In 1994, the government's independent counsel finally issued a report on Iran-Contra, informing the rest of America that the Reagan administration had been breaking the law and lying to Congress during the affair. By then, however, it was all blood under the bridge.

The counterculture's distrust of our government had grown over the years. After the assassination of John F. Kennedy, many of us began to believe that Washington had been taken over by secret, sinister forces. How else to explain the fact that we supported repressive, antidemocratic leaders around the world—Diem, Ky, and Thieu in Vietnam, Marcos in the Phillipines, Pinochet in Chile, Somoza in Nicaragua, Arbenz in Guatemala, the Shah in Iran, Saddam Hussein in Iraq, "Papa Doc" Duvalier in Haiti, Manuel Noriega in Panama. Our military gave their regimes weapons and instruction, and the CIA trained their secret police and death squads, helping them eliminate their opponents in the name of fighting communism. By the '90s most of these dictators had fallen, and we received official confirmation of their corruption, and usually of some level of U.S. support and complicity.

I did not have three thousand pairs of shoes. I had one thousand and sixty.

IMELDA MARCOS

As the cold war came undone and national security secrets were declassified, many of our wildest conspiracy theories were proven true. For instance, in the autumn of 1993, newly released documents revealed that in the early '60s the CIA had been in cahoots with the Mafia to assassinate Fidel Castro. Their schemes included exploding cigars, a Paper Mate pen with a poisoned syringe attached, and a plan to spray Castro with an LSD-like substance. They were even experimenting with a chemical that would make Castro's beard fall off. The CIA never did like beards, or leftist leaders like Castro.

Of course, a case could be made against the CIA for their incompetence throughout the Cold War. The Agency did a poor job of predicting the strength or timing of popular uprisings in Cuba, Vietnam (especially the Tet Offensive), Nicaragua, the Phillipines, and Iran, to cite a few notable examples. Perhaps the CIA agents were too busy propping up the rulers of these countries. In addition, disclosures made public in 1992 reveal that throughout the '80s the CIA was lying to Congress about the strength of the Soviet military and economy. Now that the Cold War is over, maybe the CIA should just be decommissioned. Start a new CIA, if necessary; one that at least believes in democracy.

There was plenty of despair in my America during the '80s. My friends and I watched the Reagan and Bush administrations orchestrate an era of deregulated greed which led to the further conglomerating and incorporating of our economy, the malling of our cities, the destruction of our ecosystems, and the further loss of our nation's soul. It was especially sad, and even frightening, to see so many Americans infatuated with Reagan, eagerly joining in the binge.

But there was little enthusiasm for protest, and all we could do was try to keep up our own spirits. To commemorate Reagan's second innauguration, a coalition of Bay Area progressives staged the "Berkeley Anti-Reagan Festival," or BARF. One game on the midway offered people a chance to "Break Nancy Reagan's China," by throwing baseballs at replicas of her kitchenware. Another booth challenged folks to "Pin the Missile on the Elephant." In response to the Christian fundamentalism that permeated through the Reagan government, a few people walked among the crowds at the BARF festival carrying "Anti-God" posters.

One of the slogans of the Vietnam antiwar movement had been "Make love, not war." On the day of Ronald Reagan's second inauguration, after it had become clear that the nation was still in thrall to Mammon, I told my radio audience that the radical slogan for the '80s should be, "Make love, not money." Herb Caen quoted me in his column in the San Francisco Chronicle and suggested that I put the slogan on a T-shirt and try to make some profit from it.

In the '80s I occasionally called my radio broadcast "The Last News Show," reflecting my sense that some kind of apocalypse was at hand. I was not alone in this feeling. The Christian fundamentalists agreed with me, and even the president of the United States and members of his administration talked about the coming end of days. (Reagan's Secretary of Interior James Watt told reporters, "I don't know how many more generations we can count on before the Lord returns.") The environmental and new age movements have been driven by apocalyptic notions, and lately it seems that most people—at some level of awareness—sense that we are at a critical moment in human history.

While I personally don't think we're going to destroy ourselves anytime soon, it sure feels that way sometimes. The litany of ongoing disasters is familiar: global warming, ozone depletion, deforestation, desertification, droughts, plagues, famines, toxic pollution, and economic decline.

Too many people is the main problem. When you consider that everybody's got their own problems, it becomes obvious that the more people there are in the world, the more problems there will be. Somebody should have figured this out a long time ago.

As our difficulties multiply and the clock ticks down to the millenium, sightings of both Elvis and Jesus have increased. Religious fundamentalists take to the streets and the airwaves, pointing to the passages in their holy books that confirm our darkest visions. "The apocalypse is here, folks, right on schedule." You can read all about it in the Book of Revelations. The Mayan codices and the Hopi elders also tell us that the time of upheaval is here. It's also in the Hindu scriptures, which place us in the middle of an age known as the Kali Yuga. This time of destruction is ruled over by Kali Ma, a goddess who is traditionally depicted with blood dripping from her fangs and holding a necklace of male skulls.

Is it only coincidence that brings these dire warnings from different cultures together? What if these predictions are right, and the whole planet is about to go bonkers? Maybe my new age friends and I shouldn't be trying to "be here now." Maybe we should all be trying to get the hell out of here...now!

It is possible that we are at one of those big moments in history, the dying that must precede the resurrection. It could also be that we are suffering from a case of "millenial fever." In the West, where our own history has become our religion, we give great importance to divisions of time (eras, decades, centuries), and we give special weight to those dates ending with three zeros. In the years approaching the last millienium, 1000 A.D., there were also dire warnings of the end of days, a response which now seems like nothing but superstition.

There may be no real reason to get so upset. After all, we survived the last ice age, Attila the Hun, the bubonic plague, countless thousands of wars, Hitler, Kissinger, volcanoes, tidal waves, hurricanes, and, so far, the nuclear arms race. Why should the species fail now, especially when we are at the height of our tool-making abilities? Do we face a crisis so different in scope and kind that our past record does not apply? Can we no longer rely on our accumulated skills to figure a way out of this mess?

And what if we can't? I am usually motivated (or forced by instinct) to try to preserve my species, but it might be for the best if humans were sacrificed for the sake of the rest of the life of the planet. Certainly we are the most destructive of life-forms, and, furthermore, we put ourselves through more unnecessary pains than any other species, at least as far as we know. Do you think a slug ever suffers frustration from the slowness of its pace? Does your dog worry about death or whether or not his license should be renewed? Does a bear or a salmon ever yearn for transcendence? Of course other animals seem to feel fear and hunger—the elementary forms of dissatisfaction—but only humans have made desire into a creed. Like a security blanket, we cling tightly to our dissatisfaction. What we have is never enough.

> *In America...I have seen the freest and best educated of men in the circumstances the happiest to be found in the world; yet it seemed to me that a cloud habitually hung on their brow, and they seemed serious and almost sad in their pleasure...because they never stop thinking of the good things they have not got.*
>
> ALEXIS DE TOCQUEVILLE

Even though I love my juicer and my flush toilet, I seriously doubt whether humans living in the affluence of America or Europe are that much happier than those who lived in ancient Mesopotamia, or those who lived in tribes on the great plains of North America thousands of years ago. They may not have been as comfortable physically, but those cultures had their belief systems intact and felt certain about the meaning of life and death. Besides, in every age, expectations are scaled to possibilities; life is always a mixture of joys and sorrows, and one god seems to be no better than another when it comes to handing out justice and mercy.

In spite of it all, I can still make a good case for the survival of humanity. Without us the earth would lose some of its beauty, simply because there would be no one around to proclaim it beautiful. Let's face it, the other animals are not romantics. If humans were gone who would adore the seashore or gaze lovingly at the sunsets or groom the horses or hug the dogs or write odes to the lillies? Without us the earth would just be itself and nothing more. Of course, if we were gone it would eliminate the need for life insurance.

I certainly do hope we survive if for no other purpose than what philosopher-musician John Cage cited as a reason to live longer—just to see what will happen. An even better reason is that humans seem to be the only species that has the ability to laugh at itself. For that sound alone, we should try to prolong this comedy of errors.

Throughout the Reagan-Bush years, metaphysical sanity was much easier to come by than the political kind, and I found myself going deeper into meditation practice and becoming more involved in Buddhist activities. The community of meditators was a place of refuge for me, an island of peace in a MAD world, where I could gather with friends to share laughter, sorrow, and silence. I also believed that in some way meditation was a method of resistance. As the Tao Te Ching says, "Yield and overcome." As to the Republican juggernaut, the same book informed me, "That which goes against the Tao comes to an early end." I was waiting it out.

In 1983, at the request of meditation teacher and friend Joseph Goldstein, I started a magazine for Buddhist insight meditators in the West. Another friend, Barbara Gates, agreed to be coeditor, and we decided to call the journal *Inquiring Mind*, a quality the Buddha encouraged in his disciples. (Not to be confused with the *National Enquirer*, or its slogan, "Inquiring Minds Want to Know.") From the beginning we were determined to keep the journal eclectic and at least a little irreverent, which I think we manage to do in spite of the inevitable disputes that arise among insight meditators over issues of spiritual correctness.

Once we published a forum of meditation teachers debating whether we are already enlightened and meditating only to be reminded of that fact, or not yet enlightened and meditating in order to reach that state. Ideological discussions like this are a healthy sign that Buddhism has established itself in America. Soon we hope the teachers will tackle the question of how many bodhisattvas can dance on the head of a pin.

The Reagan era drove me deeper into meditation, and, at the same time, called me out into the world. This split in myself was not new. Ever since I began meditating, I have felt a tension between my political impulses and my Buddhist understanding of ultimate reality. Sometimes I've felt like two different people with disparate beliefs. Perhaps the tension finally became too great, and I had to seek its resolution.

I was not alone in my efforts—a definite shift began to take place in Western Buddhism in the 1980s. Many teachers emphasized more engagement in the world, or began working more with "loving-kindness" meditation and practices of compassion. A few started teaching meditation to groups of environmental activists, or worked with AIDS patients, prisoners, or the dying. The Dalai Lama and Vietnamese monk Thich Nhat Hanh became heros in the West, as exemplars of "engaged Buddhism." A few prominent Buddhist leaders started a worldwide organization called the Buddhist Peace Fellowship, and others offered mediation services to groups or governments in conflict. Perhaps after a decade or so of deconstructing ourselves, it was time to test whatever realization we had achieved in the fires of the world.

In 1982 I went back to India with the intention of exploring the link between politics and mysticism. I wanted to talk to some gurus about nuclear war and the environment. In the midst of all that cosmic wisdom, maybe there was a secret oral teaching on social action, a Hindu or Buddhist brand of liberation theology.

On previous trips to Asia I had carried a tape recorder with me, but usually set it aside while I tried to erase the tapes in my head. I had used my trusty Sony a few times—to record the street sounds of Calcutta's urban chaos, and the wild, devotional chanting in Hindu temples—but on this trip I contracted to do two documentaries for National Public Radio. One of them was to be on the legacy of Mahatma Gandhi, and the other was a report on the International Transpersonal Psychology Conference, held that year in Bombay.

Transpersonal is a new wing of psychology, put together by the more adventuresome psycho-spiritual explorers in the West. Some of my best friends call themselves transpersonal psychologists, and they seem to practice a kind of experiential, neo-Jungian shamanism. They investigate nonordinary and heightened states of consciousness, the psychology of mysticism, and the uses of myth and ritual, all the while inventing new methods of healing and "soul-making," as Jung called it. Simply put, they are trying to revise our definition of who we are and what we might become.

The Transpersonal Psychology Conference at the President Hotel in Bombay turned out to be a kind of East-West lovefest. All sorts of swamis and lamas came to hear the Western scholars praise and corraborate their ancient traditions, and the Westerners simply begged them to reveal more of it. The twain was finally meeting.

Stanislav Grof, one of the founders of transpersonal psychology, talked about the technique of holotropic breathwork as an avenue to cosmic consciousness; Fritjof Capra described the correlation between science and mysticism; physicist David Bohm offered his "implicate order" as a new name for the cosmic Oneness; Rabbi Zalman Schacter spoke on his concept of "eco-kosher" and about the Jewish understanding of the absolute. When I interviewed Schacter, he said told me that the Buddha's first noble truth of suffering was discovered independantly by Jews, expressed primarily through the "oy vey" mantra.

Mother Teresa spoke at the conference, and the Dalai Lama was scheduled to appear but fell sick at the last minute. A couple of uninvited barefoot sadus and swamis tried to crash the event. They ended up sitting out on the lawn of the hotel, offering their morsels of wisdom to anybody not satisfied with the cosmic supper being served up inside.

After the conference ended, I started traveling around India to gather tape for the documentary about Gandhi. A quarter century after his assassination, all that was left of the Ghandian movement were some scattered ashrams and community centers where a few young social workers experimented with appropriate technologies and cottage industries, while older veterans of Gandhi's independance campaign sat around and told stories about their exploits and early idealism. These remains seemed to be an Indian version of Berkeley radicalism in the '80s.

Part of my search for Gandhi's legacy took me to Bodhgaya, the same village where I had learned how to meditate. During previous trips to India, I was too busy not thinking to think much about Gandhi. It turned out that right down the street from where I had been meditating in 1970 was an ashram devoted to carrying on Gandhi's work, ministering to the needs of the poor and trying to hold on to the Mahatma's vision for a sane society.

The Samanvaya Ashram in Bodhgaya was run by a man named Dwarko, a stocky, intelligent Bengali in his late fifties. He had been working for thirty years here in Bihar State, one of the poorest regions in India. During that time he had supervised the construction of thirteen new villages for peasants, most of whom were members of the so-called "rat-eaters" caste. These people did not even have rice to eat for more than six months out of the year, and often were forced to eat leaves and roots. These were garnish for one of their main sources of protein: rat meat. Almost all of these villagers lived below the *Indian* poverty line, which is the equivalent of about five dollars a month. "We started from minus zero," Dwarko says of the people he works with, "and we still haven't reached zero."

The villages Dwarko helped build for these people were part of Gandhi's plan for India after independance, his so-called "constructive program." Like most people, I had been aware of the Mahatma's committment to nonviolence, but I hadn't known about his program for "village socialism" in India, or his critique of capitalism, or his ideas about education and ecology. In fact, Gandhi had a comprehensive design for a cooperative society, which is not talked about very much in India, or anywhere else in the world for that matter. Neither communists nor capitalists wanted anything to do with the Mahatma's idea of a decentralized, spiritually-based "village republic." As Dwarko and other Gandhian workers explained it to me, I was amazed at how similar the Mahatma's ideas were to those of my eco-philosopher friends in the American counterculture. Like them, Gandhi had rejected the twentieth century.

After independence, India's politicians ignored Gandhi's constructive program. They were infatuated with the West, and wanted to turn their nation into a modern industrial state. Gandhi had lived in London at the turn of century and saw the slums of Liverpool, and he concluded that industrial capitalism was an evil. He saw that it led to the concentration of wealth and power, the creation of big cities full of displaced people, and a consequent breakdown of ethics, spiritual values, family, and community. Gandhi understood that the problem was partly a matter of size and scale:

> Society based on nonviolence can only consist of groups settled in small units or villages, where voluntary co-operation is the condition of dignified and peaceful existence. This end can only be achieved under decentralization. Centralization cannot be sustained and defended without force. It is not unreasonable to presume from the state of the West that its cities, its monster factories and huge armaments are so intimately interrelated that the one cannot exist without the other. The nearest approach to civilization based upon non-violence is the erstwhile village republic of India.

Gandhi was new age even before there was one. He believed that "small is beautiful," and advocated appropriate technology as an alternative, and not just a stepping stone to large-scale industry and mass production. He also believed that all living beings are equally sacred, making him one of the world's first deep ecologists. He called his deep ecology "biological nonviolence."

Gandhi knew that people would have to sacrifice in order to achieve a new society; in his own words he called for "voluntary simplicity." With his life, however, Gandhi set standards of simplicity that few Americans would even try to meet. He once visited the King of England wearing only a loincloth, shawl, and sandals. Later, when questioned about the propriety of his attire, Gandhi said, "It was quite alright. The King was wearing enough for both of us." When he died, Gandhi left only a few personal possessions: a figurine of the see no evil, hear no evil, speak no evil monkeys, his spectacles and walking staff, a few pieces of homespun clothing, and his spinning wheel. As rural and old-fashioned as his vision may appear to those of us immersed in modernity, we may yet find ourselves asking Gandhi's advice for ways to get out of the complicated tangles of our global village.

The Dalai Lama shares Gandhi's understanding of social problems. By chance, I was staying in Bodhgaya when the Tibetan leader arrived to give Buddhist teachings to his people living in exile in that part of India. I wanted to include the Dalai Lama in my documentary, and since this was before he was awarded the Nobel Peace Prize, I was able to arrange a meeting with him fairly easily.

My first question to His Holiness, as many Buddhists call him, was, "What do you think Tibetans have to teach us in the West." He thought for a moment, and then replied, "How to make *sampa*, Tibetan-style butter tea." Then he burst into laughter. Later in our talk he told me his now familiar line, "My religion is kindness." That may sound simplistic, but if you practice it like the Dalai Lama does, it becomes a radical doctrine. He even calls the Chinese—who have stolen his country, and destroyed his peoples' temples and monasteries—his friends.

I was also taken by the Dalai Lama's simple statement, "My economics is sufficiency." Enough is enough. That's exactly the same idea as sustainability, just put a little differently. It's also the basis of Gandhi's village socialism. The Dalai Lama believes, as did Gandhi, that after certain needs are met, true happiness comes not from material wealth but from the cultivation of peace, both inside and outside. That seems to be the bottom line of spiritual politics.

My last stop in India was at the Gandhi memorial in New Delhi. At the entrance, Gandhi's talisman was carved in stone: "Whenever you are in doubt, or when the self becomes too much with you, try the following expedient. Recall the face of the poorest and the most helpless person whom you have ever seen, and then ask yourself if the step you contemplate is going to be of any use to him." Reading it, I thought of how far removed the world is from the Gandhian ideal. But as Gandhi said, "Satisfaction lies in the effort, not in the attainment. Full effort is full victory."

When I returned from India, I produced a documentary that drew on parallels between Gandhi's ideas and those of the new age and environmental movements. The connection had been confirmed for me at a Gandhian ashram in Warda, India, where I found a dog-eared copy of the Whole Earth Catalogue on the director's desk. In my radio program, however, I tried to downplay the fact that Gandhi's ideas were largely ignored in India. If they didn't play in Punjab, then how could they play in Peoria? But as Gandhi once said, probably with a twinkle in his eye, "Truth does not become error just because nobody believes it."

At the Gandhi memorial in New Delhi, I violated the rules by snapping my own picture of a framed photograph of the Mahatma with Charlie Chaplin, the two of them laughing together. Both were my heroes, and I wanted to place this image on my personal alter of allies and inspirations. Some years later, while writing an article about the influences that led me to Buddhism, I realized what an odd assortment of heroes I have accumulated. Scientists, comedians, mystics—all feeding different parts of myself. Trying to find some connections between them led to my first book, *Crazy Wisdom*.

In the book, I trace the threads that link Gandhi's voluntary poverty to Charlie Chaplin's tramp, the Buddha's thin smile with Alfred E. Neuman's wide grin, Mark Twain's great putdown of Christianity with Lily Tomlin's search for intelligent life in the universe. The threads unite existentialists and dadaists with Zen and Taoist masters, and emerge from the crazy quilt to tie off at their beatniks and hippie children. My friend Paul Krassner said that the book served as "the missing link between sit-down meditation and stand-up comedy."

Crazy Wisdom was partly born in the workshops that I began teaching with Paul in the mid 1980s. A friend started getting us booked into new age venues such as Esalen Institute in Big Sur and Hollyhock Farm in British Columbia. The catalog descriptions announce that our workshop will not necessarily help you to be funny, but rather to "see funny." We also promise to prove that the cosmic and comic are One.

In general, I am the straight man, giving a philosophical context to the subject of humor, telling Zen and Coyote stories and talking about the differences between clowns, jesters, tricksters, and fools. Paul prevents the class from getting too serious. He was cofounder of the Yippies, the Youth International Party, and is editor of the infamous *Realist* magazine, known for its irreverance and outlandish conspiracy theories. His autobiography was entitled *Confessions of a Raving Unconfined Nut*, which is what the FBI called him in their files.

In one of our workshop exercises we divide the class into small groups and ask them to invent their own religions. (That's what has been happening out here in the West anyway at the close of the millenium.) Each group then puts on a skit that reveals their new deities and beliefs. These become little rituals of irreverence and defiance, exorcisms, shared expressions of disdain or dismay over the lives we lead. One group worshipped washing machines (cleanliness is next to godliness) by celebrating the different cycles: getting soaked, becoming agitated, and finally spinning around like dervishes. Others have worshipped their life insurance premiums, automobile tires, and of course, the almighty credit card, which teaches the laws of karma in every monthly statement of truth.

Lately we are having people in our classes invent their own forms of government as well. We are hoping that something workable comes along soon.

From the comic perspective, humanity's current dilemma might best be portrayed by Charlie Chaplin as "everyman." The scene opens with Charlie in a room, enthusiastically building an engine. He is happy and proud of himself as he dances around his invention, deftly putting the final pieces in place and tightening up the screws. At last, after taking out his handkerchief and, with a flourish, wiping off the last bit of dust, Charlie pushes the button and the engine springs to life. But his elation only lasts for a minute, because the machine suddenly begins a jerking motion and starts belching out smoke. The room begins to fill up with clouds of smoke, and the engine starts lurching about on its own. Charlie rushes to the window but discovers that it is stuck, then rushes to the door but that won't open either. The scene closes with his forlorn face pressed up against the window, miming a plea for help.

As the French philosopher Denis Diderot once said, "What a fine comedy this world would be, if one did not have to play a part in it." Unfortunately, we are not in the audience for this show. We are the clowns, getting ourselves into deep trouble with our so-called ingenuity (engine-uity, en-genius) and our unjustifiable pride. "Hey, Rube! The engine's going out of control, and the smoke is getting thicker!"

We clowns don't catch on too quickly either. Instead of trying to turn the engine off, we keep building more engines, burning more oil, and creating more and more smoke. And more and more people want engines of their own. Scientists point to human overpopulation as the primary environmental problem, but what about the ominous proliferation of oil-burning vehicles? In 1950 there were 50 million cars and trucks on the planet; today there are 500 million! The human population has only doubled since 1950, but the vehicle population has increased by a factor of ten. And now the Chinese and the Eastern Europeans and Brazilians all want private cars. Are you going to be the one to hop in your Chevy or Honda and go tell them that it's too late, we have already used up most of the oil on the planet and most of the oxygen as well? "Sorry folks, from now on everybody will have to learn how to skateboard."

Someone ought to tell the OPEC ministers how unliveable their deserts will be if global warming continues, and suggest that it might be wise if they cut back on oil production for a while. "Just dole out that ol, dinosaur juice slowly, boys, or else we will all be following those tiny-brained giants down the road to ruin-car-nation!" And isn't it ironic to think that by burning up the remains of the Jurassic, we might be replicating the atmospheric conditions that extinquished that burst of life.

No matter what gets said in official circles, the Persian Gulf War of 1991 was fought primarily for the sake of cheap oil. We were told that we were fighting to liberate Kuwait, but if freedom is the guiding light of American and European foreign policy, why didn't we try long ago to save Tibet from the Chinese? There was simply nothing in it for us. Tibet's most valuable resource is Buddhist meditation and the practices of love and compassion. Unlike oil, our leaders don't consider these to be part of our vital national interests.

There certainly does seem to be some glitch in the old survival brain, and I'm afraid it will take even bigger traumas to wake us up. The worldwide economic recession might be a partial antidote, a kind of compulsory eco-consciousness. Let's euphemize (and alliterate) and from now on call our major economic downturns "economically enforced evolution."

Back in the 1970s, there was a short-lived new age idea called "voluntary simplicity." Well, not enough people volunteered. Now we're facing compulsory simplicity. When California's then governor, Jerry Brown, tried to promote the idea of "lowered expectations" it didn't fly, maybe because people didn't perceive simplicity as being any fun. I think the counterculture needs to hire a better public relations firm. Peace and simplicity have to be sold as sexy.

In the West, fun has become synonymous with intensity. At rock-and-roll concerts, the sound is always turned up to decibel levels which automatically cause the blood vessels in the body to constrict. The resulting tension is labeled "fun." Violent and scary movies work on us in the same way, pulling us directly into the moment, driving everything else out of our minds for a while, giving us a heightened sense of being alive. Maybe that is why rock concerts and big screen movie spectaculars have become our surrogate religious ceremonies. Hollywood is Holy-wood, and we are looking for baptism in the flow of images, our way into other worlds. People ridicule the Moonies, but most of us are "screenies," and when we go into the darkened theater or sit down in our living rooms, the Reverend Screen projects the myths we live by.

Kill your television.

BUMPER STICKER, 1990

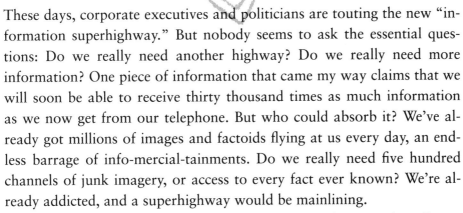

These days, corporate executives and politicians are touting the new "information superhighway." But nobody seems to ask the essential questions: Do we really need another highway? Do we really need more information? One piece of information that came my way claims that we will soon be able to receive thirty thousand times as much information as we now get from our telephone. But who could absorb it? We've already got millions of images and factoids flying at us every day, an endless barrage of info-mercial-tainments. Do we really need five hundred channels of junk imagery, or access to every fact ever known? We're already addicted, and a superhighway would be mainlining.

Instead, maybe we should build more rest stops. Let people pull over and check out a reality that is not virtual. Walk around on unreconstructed earth for awhile. See trees in their natural habitat.

GO OUT AND MAKE SOME OF YOUR OWN

Let's encourage people to get outside more, take back their streets, join a community. Too much info-tainment pushes common sense out of the mind, and wisdom out of the heart. Too much imagery makes us jumpy, nervous, and disatisfied. Instead of getting on the new information superhighway, maybe instead we should take the Beatles' advice and, at least for a little while every day, "Turn off your mind, relax, and float downstream..."

> *Maybe the Beat Generation, which is the offspring of the Lost Generation, is just another step toward that last, pale generation, which will not know the answer either. In any case, indications are that its effect has taken root in American culture.*
>
> JACK KEROUAC

The 1980s shook my faith in any counterculture's viability, and made me question my own vision of the future. I began to ask myself whether the Eastern spiritual practices, alternative paradigms, and eco-sustainable lifestyles have any real future. Is the new age nothing more than nostalgia for a human past that never existed, and a future that does not include sentimentality? Maybe my friends and I are just too idealistic, and upset because the world does not live up to our expectations? Maybe the high-tech capitalist global economy will do just fine, and humanity will come to a new equilibrium that has nothing to do with our funkier version of how evolution should take place.

My favorite Eastern aphorism is from the Taoist sage, Chuang Tzu, who says "Those who know they are fools are not the biggest fools." That's my truth, and my cop-out. I don't presume to know what's going to happen. And while I don't believe its time yet for the last news show, I *do* believe we are going to spend a good part of the next century paying for this one.

LEARNING HOW TO LOVE

Chapter Eleven

THE WORLD
ANYWAY

Oh, what a catastrophe, what maiming of love when it was made a personal, merely personal feeling, taken away from the rising and the setting of the sun, and cut off from the magic connection of the solstice and equinox! This is what is the matter with us, we are bleeding at the roots, because we are cut off from the earth and sun and stars, and love is a grinning mockery, because, poor blossom, we plucked it from its stem on the tree of Life, and expected it to keep on blooming in our civilized vase on the table.

D. H. LAWRENCE

The most difficult task I have set for myself is to fuse my head and my heart. Not just to think about loving, but to love. It's a matter of bringing what I learn in my meditation practice back out, as the yogis say, "into the marketplace." To *embody* the teachings. The problem has something to do with metabolism. To mellow out, or not to mellow out? Maybe *that* is the question.

Several times during the '70s and '80s, I went back to India just to meditate for a month or two, and I also attended ten-day silent retreats in the United States. During these practice periods, I would regain some mental clarity and perspective on myself, or my non-self, as it were. Usually, my heart would open as well, and I would begin to feel a sense of expansiveness, full of love for the world again.

Then I would return to my "real" life, slowly but surely revving up to speed for work and play in America. I'd go back to various jobs in media, follow the news, get current with the latest trends, and before long my concentration and calm would begin to dissipate. I could almost feel the old cynicism about life returning, like a cloud spreading in my mind. It didn't feel good, and I'd try to fight it off, but usually could only manage a draw. To make matters worse, some old Jewish guilt-gear would also lock into place, and I'd criticize myself for not being able to hold on to what I perceived as a sublime state of consciousness.

When things got too hard for me, or when the news made me cringe with fear or sadness, I would retreat to the nihilistic side of the Buddha's teachings. That's the part about seeing through the illusion of all manifest forms and detaching oneself from the world. I would hide there, synchronizing my cynicism with that zero place where all our endeavors come to nothing.

The other side of the Buddha's teachings is where you learn to love all of life, empty though it may be. But those are teachings of the heart, and I think for years my meditation practice remained too much of a head trip, as we used to say. While Buddhism had answered my desire for metaphysical sanity, a Western-style emotional awakening helped bring me back to earth.

There is a lot of work going on in Western schools of experiential psychology to get peoples' emotional juices flowing. The Reichians and gestalt leaders have invented systematic methods of blowing out the too-civilized circuits, and the neo-Jungians are now using myth and ritual to mine our grief and joy. Perhaps these practices have developed in response to the fact that we live too much in our heads.

I became involved with one of these psycho-spiritual healing processes when Jack Kornfield asked me to help him teach Buddhist meditation at a holotropic breathwork retreat. Holotropic breathwork is a process developed by Stanislav and Christina Grof, who seem to know as much as anybody in the West about altered states of consciousness. Stanislav did pioneering work with the theraputic uses of LSD, and, with his wife, Christina, discovered that in a controlled setting, sessions of intensive breathing could provide people with access to similar nonordinary states. While leading thousands through this process, the Grofs have found that people gain access to difficult memories and resolve past trauma; great stores of tension and suppressed emotion are released. It is also possible through holotropic breathwork to experience archetypal imagery and energies; some people even feel a kind of mystical unity with all things.

During the breathwork sessions, people lie on mattresses on the floor, breathing deeply and rapidly for two or more hours at a time. Evocative music is played, which builds in intensity until it peaks, usually at the same time as all sorts of imagery and emotion. The room becomes filled with wails, sighs, laughter, shouts, howls, and growls.

I have done the breathwork several times, and the process often seems to move me out of my personal story. During one session, for instance, I felt a surge of anger at myself for mistakes I had made, but after a while that turned into a kind of primal anger directed at nothing less than human fate. Laying there on my mattress, some kind of warrior inside me began fighting a heroic battle against all the delusion and suffering of the world.

There were moments of joy in the breathwork as well, and whole sessions of energetic dancing, as my body shook on the mattress in semi-controlled abandon. At times I felt myself to be an animal, my hands turning into claws, my neck and torso moving in some imitation of prowling tiger or coyote. It sounds corny to say it, but the breathwork did indeed get me in touch with my animal nature. I'm a mid-sized mammal.

Breathwork is the kind of medicine that environmentalists would prescribe. It helps put people back in their bodies and back on the earth. Like other tools made popular in the new age—tarot, the enneagram, or astrology—the breathwork is also a way to step out of binding individualism. You identify with a common personality pattern, and take your place in an archetypal human community.

In sacred space people suffer what they need to suffer, and fear to suffer.

CARL JUNG

Ritual is another ally in my struggle with cynicism. More and more, I find myself drawn to ritual events—happy and sad ones, new and used. Finding some way to honor life and the world helps me to fend off despair and my nagging nihilism. So I light some incense, call out the gods, try to usher the seasons in and out. Through ritual I'm learning to bow down to this manifest world, to see it as the big everything rather than the big nothing.

One ritual that really grabbed me took place at a gathering of men. Yes I did some of that, too. If I had asked my body, of course, my genetalia would have told me which gender I am. Balls? Check. Penis? Check. But my identity as "a man" was something I never considered until the womens' movement came along, and then the mens' movement. Just as in the '60s I had begun to think of myself as part of a generation, in the '80s I suddenly found myself joining a gender. Deconstruction rules.

In 1977 I had interviewed Robert Bly for my radio show on KSAN. At the time Bly had not yet focused on men's issues. He was then mostly concerned about our inability, as individuals and as a nation, to grieve, or to face what Jung and others called the "shadow." Bly said that our shadow always has something important to teach us, a concept that reminded me of the famous line from the radio mystery show—"The shadow knows."

Bly was opposed to the emerging new age spirituality. When I asked him about meditation, he told me that young Americans who were turning to Eastern mysticism were going in the wrong direction. He said that Americans did not need to transcend, to go upward, but instead, needed to descend, to touch down on earth and go into the grief buried deep in every American psyche. Bly was passionate about it. "When I meet spiritual people in this country, they're just too damn cheerful," he said. "The American way is to be cheerful, not to talk about the darkness or the crimes. We have never grieved for the Indians who we slaughtered and whose land we stole, we have never grieved for the Vietnam War. If the Zen Center in San Francisco would hold a public ceremony to grieve for the Vietnam War, then I could believe that spirituality was taking hold in this country."

Thirteen years later, Bly himself organized a public ceremony at Fort Mason in San Francisco to mourn the Vietnam War. I was among the five thousand people who smeared ashes on their face, and joined in a community wailing over a conflict that had ended almost a quarter century before.

But the ritual that really grabbed me, and grieved me as well, took place at a week-long men's reatreat in a redwood forest camp in Mendocino, California. After some arm-twisting, Jack Kornfield (again) convinced me to attend this gathering, which he was helping to lead along with psychologist James Hillman, mythologist Michael Meade, and African medicine man and ritualist Maladoma Somé.

After registration I was asked to chose a clan that I would belong to for the week: Red Deer, Raven, or Trout. My cynicism flag went up. This sounded too much like boy-scout camp. I finally decided to become a raven, because they are tricksters in many mythological traditions, and I thought I could play that familiar role. However, the ravens at this men's retreat were given a somewhat different agenda, written out for us on our clan assignment sheet:

> *The ravens catch the shadows of men and walk among the bones of the battlefields. They never neglect the darkness. Bearing hard, truthful messages from the invisible, they nourish the lonely soul with gifts of intuition, for their intense sharpness sees the jewels others miss.*

It was difficult for me to find the raven within. When I asked myself why it was so hard, all I could answer was, "beCAWS, beCAWS." As the week progressed, however, some elements of the retreat began to work for me. Especially the grieving ritual.

Maladome Somé organized the event, based on the funeral ceremonies of his West African tribe, the Dagara. Maladome is a fully initiated Dagara medicine man whose elders sent him to be educated in Europe and the United States. After meeting him, Bly and Meade recruited Maladome to help teach the men's gatherings.

During a discussion one day, Maladome told us that he had been trained by his tribal elders to see directly into people's spirits. When he first came to the United States, he said, he was frightened by the sight of so many people "who had a big hole where their necks should be." Walking around New York City, he also saw many "ghosts of the ungrieved dead," as he called them. Before his second trip to the West, he asked his elders to remove this power to see spirits.

As we prepared for the ritual, James Hillman explained, "Grief in our culture takes the posture of solemnity. People just stand around in the church or at the cemetery, and it's all bowed heads and muffled sobs. Visually, it resembles shame as much as grief." According to Hillman, the grief gets stuck inside. It doesn't move, and it poisons the soul.

The grieving ceremony took place on a field between two stands of redwoods. At one end of the field was "the village," the gathering spot, where men played drums and sang a sorrowful chant. On the other end of the field was a sanctified area bordered by stones, which represented "the other world." In the West African ritual this was where the dead were layed out, but for our purposes this became an area that contained all our losses—not only the imaginary bodies of those close to us who had died, but also the lovers who had left us, the America that had disappointed us, the Vietnam War dead, our dying cities, the sorrow of all our enormous twentieth-century confusion. We symbolically placed these losses in the sanctified area, and then gathered in the "village" to join the drumming and chanting.

The ritual turned out to be African gestalt therapy, transplanted in North America. Its intended purpose was to break open our hearts, and for most of us it did. In the West African villages the mourners attempt to throw themselves over into the sanctified area, to follow their loved ones into the other world. At the men's gathering we were told that when we felt grief arise, to walk or dance or even run across the field over to the shrine area. Once there we were to "hurl our grief into the other world."

It is difficult to create a new ritual. It requires agreement by a particular community that certain acts and words have a shared sacred meaning. Without time and tradition to give significance to a ceremony, whether it be celebration or mourning, the effect can feel contrived. So much depends on the participants' ability to release themselves into the mystery, and that requires a kind of foolish bravery. Sometimes I can let go, and sometimes I can't.

I resisted the grieving ritual sucessfully for an hour or so, but as I watched other men begin to weep, I started to feel the sadness inside myself. At first I felt a little embarrassed to sob in front of other men, but as I let it happen, my sadness soon changed from something personal into sadness for everybody's sadness. I felt the inevitable pain of our bodies, subject to sickness and certain death; the ongoing sorrow of losing our loved ones; the awareness of a troubled world with its vanishing species and burgeoning human population; that, and all the ordinary suffering humans go through in any era.

Aside from the emotional catharsis it provided, the grieving ritual made me aware of the fact that I usually keep a certain distance from my emotions. That stance has cut me off, not only from suffering, for which I am always thankful, but also from a degree of intimacy with the world. When I close my heart to protect myself from sorrow, no matter how slightly, it also gets closed to the emotions of love and joy. As always, for any taste to exist at all, you must have both the bitter and the sweet.

I realized as well that I was sometimes hiding inside my meditation practice, using it to maintain my distance, to stay an outsider. Others who I have spoken to agree that the equanimity developed in meditation can sometimes turn into sterile detachment. Instead of feeling more human after cracking open the shell of ego, it is also possible to feel ex-human. Like the Buddhist heart-chakra practices of loving kindness and compassion, the grieving ritual seemed to work as a corrective to meditative detachment.

The men's reatreat wasn't just about grief. It included back-and-forth Sufi-style poetry readings, with renditions of Yeats, Jeffers, Blake, Li Po, Ryokan, and Rumi—especially Rumi—the *awe*some Sufi mystic-poet whose verse has become the bible of new ritualists and spiritualists.

Over the course of the retreat, Michael Meade told us Celtic tales of archetypal fools and heros, full of symbolic imagery around the great themes of life and death. Meade says that these images allow people to connect their personal story to the mythic story. Then, he explains, "there is this immediate relief from the personal. The load is partially carried by the story. Secondly, a community occurs. What people used to call "communitas." Everyone winds up connected to the same story, even though they may be connected in different ways."

By the time the retreat was over, I did feel part of a community, however temporary. The same thing happens at meditation retreats, and at other workshops I've attended as well. As James Hillman says, "Community is sitting at the same mystery."

I see other similarities between the work with ritual and myth and meditation practice. In both there is an attempt to step out of one's individual drama, and into wider perspectives and larger identities. While meditation focuses more on cosmic consciousness, the ritual work seems to move through Jungian archetypal realms toward a species or biological consciousness. Both practices remind us that we are all united in this moment of evolution, standing on the same plateau of history, sharing the common limits of our DNA. Both myth and meditation are balms for our age.

Working with myth and ritual can also have its downside. Over the years, for instance, my archetypal house seems to have become a bit crowded. I have Greek gods and Celtic knights and dieties from Tibetan Buddhist mandalas and old rabbis with Torahs all dancing around together in my head. Of course, I contain multitudes, just as Whitman and all of us do, and I have enjoyed getting acquainted with some of these characters. Still, it can be confusing. When I go over to my little private altar in the morning, I find a stately Buddha, a laughing Buddha, a picture of the monkey god Hannuman, a couple of Zuni fetiches, a string of Tibetan prayer beads made of human bone, each bead carved into the shape of a skull, that little photograph of Mahatma Gandhi with Charlie Chaplin, and various feathers, rocks, bells, and other ritual objects. Sometimes I ask myself, "Which of the ten thousand names of god should I invoke today?" Should I rub the laughing Buddha's stomach or say a prayer to Mother Kali, and if I do both will they cancel each other out?

Still, when all is said and done, I think I'd rather have too many gods and amulets in my life than too few. Maybe my desire to merge with the One has been answered, in some way, by the many. According to the Heart Sutra, "Form is emptiness and emptiness is form," so as long I keep the emptiness over my left shoulder, I might as well enjoy the show. As Edward Abbey said, "The world may be an illusion, but its the only illusion we've got." Having a metaphysics that makes sense is important, but poetry and imagery are what give it life. Not only do I want a spiritual practice, I want a mythology, too. Even if it is second-hand; even if it is a polyglot. Mythology keeps me in the world, and teaches me how to love it better.

THE HERE AND NOW

Part of my recovery from cynicism may have been due to the change of administrations in Washington, with the 1992 victory of Bill Clinton and Al Gore. I was not convinced that Clinton would be able to create another U.S. economic boom, but I did believe he might bring a little compassion to the American scene, and ease the pain of the decline.

For me and most of my friends, Bill Clinton is a welcome relief from Reagan and Bush, even though he doesn't exactly carry *our* sense of the sixties. After all, Clinton told *Rolling Stone* magazine that his favorite Beatle was Paul. That indicates he was also telling the truth when he said he hadn't inhaled. On top of that, Clinton chose as his campaign theme song, "Don't Stop Thinking about Tomorrow." In the sixties we were into the here and now, not "thinking about tomorrow." And instead of Fleetwood Mac, a washed up band all the way from Britain, no less, Clinton should have asked a real American band to accompany his presidency—like the Grateful Dead singing "U.S. Blues," (Let's look at our shadows, America!) or Frank Zappa and the Mothers of Invention doing their great song of inclusiveness, "We are the other people, we are the other people. You're the other people too."

Many of us were also disappointed when Clinton chose Reverend Billy Graham to give his inaugural invocation. We would have liked a more eclectic spiritual leader, or perhaps a Native American shaman who could offer a prayer to *their* Great Spirit for a change. Isn't it time we reached out, America? If Clinton wants an all-inclusive administration, it should hold true for gods and goddesses as well as people.

Nonetheless, Clinton seems to be doing the best job possible, given his moment at the helm, and it may in fact be better for everyone if he takes a somewhat moderate path toward the future. Things may have to get a little worse before they get any better. Besides, and maybe it is a function of age, but I no longer feel impatient for big, radical changes. History takes its own time, and maybe the best we can do is try to smooth its passage through our lives.

*What this country needs is
a good five cent synthesis.*

SAUL BELLOW

A political theory recently channeled itself through me, perhaps arising out of my continuing desire to find a synthesis for the various parts of myself. (I say channeled, because after watching my mind for so long in meditation, I find it difficult to take much credit for what arises there.) I call the theory Zen socialism, and it just might be the next step in the dialectic of history. Okay, you laugh. But this time we would stand Karl Marx on his head, and in that yoga posture he might be able to realize the importance of relaxation in the coming revolution. Furthermore, under Zen socialism, America would become the first nation in history to undertake an intentional decline and fall. We should call it the decline and slide.

First we must overcome our denial, and accept the fact that decline seems inevitable. When we look at history, we see empires rising and falling at fairly regular intervals, and not a single one that lives forever. An Italian poet who saw the tail end of the glory of Rome, explains the mystery of the process this way:

> *The One whose wisdom transcends everything,*
> *Fashioned the heavens and to them gave his guides,*
> *So that one pole shines out to the other,*
>
> *Apportioning, in equal measure, light.*
> *In like manner, for splendors of the world,*
> *He ordained a general minister and guide*
>
> *To shift around at times the empty wealth,*
> *From country to country and from house to house,*
> *Beyond the watchfulness of human judgement.*
>
> *And so one country rules, one lanquishes,*
> *In obedience to the verdict that she gives,*
> *Which is hidden like a snake in the grass.*

DANTE ALIGHIERI, *THE INFERNO*

The litany of fallen splendor rings through the pages of history. What happened to the Mesopotamian, Egyptian, and Babylonian empires? Today we see the great civilizations of the Mayans, Aztecs, Greeks, and Romans reduced to tourist attractions, ruins for climbing on and picture taking. Where are the powerful Chinese dynasties, and the incredibly vast Ottoman Empire? And what happened to the more recent European empires of the French, the Spanish, the Portugese, and the British? Only a few decades ago the Brits were proud to say, "The sun never sets on the British Empire." All that is left of their empire today are those few cloudy little islands in the North Atlantic, where, one could say, the sun hardly ever rises on the British Empire.

There is really only one story of empire, repeated over and over again with slight variations. In fact it seems that each empire passes on to its successor—along with the keys to the colonial treasure, of course—the blueprint and instructions for the decline and fall. The cycle, like some wild ecosystem growth, climax, and decay, is repeated over and over. In *The Rise and Fall of the Roman Empire*, authors Will and Ariel Durant report, "The essential cause of Rome's decline lay in her people, her morals, her class struggle, her failing trade, her bureaucratic despotism, her stifling taxes, her consuming wars..." Sound familiar?

But we must take heart. The end of empire might not be so terrible. We should remember that Rome didn't decline in a day. Moreover, during that decline a lot of Roman citizens probably didn't even notice it was happening. A few centuries later they started calling themselves Italians, and they seem to be doing fine today.

> *No power on earth is stronger than the United States of America today, and none will be stronger than the United States of America in the future. (Lightning strikes.)*
>
> RICHARD M. NIXON

If decline is America's fate, perhaps the best approach would be to give up without a grim, protracted struggle. In the past, the world's great powers have stubbornly tried to hold onto their imperial status and opulent lifestyles, resulting in prolonged wars and great suffering. If we could only learn from the mistakes of history we might be able to redraw the blueprint for the decline, setting an example for all future empires to follow.

Under a Zen socialist government, the United States would simply go to the United Nations and resign as a superpower, effective immediately. We would announce to the world that we would like to become just an ordinary nation. Never before has an imperial power let go with such dignity and purpose.

People usually fail when they are on the verge of success.
So give as much care to the end as to the beginning;
Then there will be no failure.

TAO TE CHING

If we are serious about resigning as a superpower, we should plan some temporary social programs to help ease the transition. I envision a five-year plan like the Chinese Communists used to set, but the Zen socialist version is called "The Great Leap Backward." The plan consists of public works projects similar to those of Roosevelt's New Deal of the 1930s; but these are programs which will help us wind *down* our economy. This is the New Age New Deal.

One of our first major challenges will be to slow ourselves down, to keep pace with declining productivity. To effect this transition, we would establish a new governmental agency, the Department of Meditation and Therapy. Deprogramming centers will be set up around the country to treat our overachievers. The DMT will start a public works project that pays people by the hour *just to work on themselves.* As people learn how to become less productive members of a less productive society, then we could move from our current condition of unemployment and overemployment to a condition of underemployment for all. By the way, the TransAmerica pyramid in San Francisco will make a perfect headquarters for the Department of Meditation and Therapy.

Another public works program will be the disassembling of America. Disassembly lines will be set up, employing people to take apart cars, melt and separate the steel back into ores, and shovel it all back into the ground. There will be plenty of temporary work breaking up unneccesary freeways and parking lots. The Army Corps of Engineers can have the job of digging up the dams they have built and letting the rivers run free again. What a glorious national task it will be!

As we take the Great Leap Backward, our citizens will also need to learn new skills. We can ask some of today's developing nations to help us out. Maybe Egypt or India could start a reverse Peace Corps and send volunteers to teach us vital skills, such as how to wash our clothes by hand, grow food in depleted soils, get by without life insurance, and most important, when and how to take the siesta. Volunteers could also mobilize a literacy campaign to go into the suburbs and teach post-literate Americans how to read and write again.

As we begin to adjust to our intentional decline, the new age will flourish. Ordinary Americans will begin growing sprouts on their kitchen windowsills, vegetable gardens will spring up on suburban lawns, and clothes will be hung out to dry from the windows of condominiums. Home remedies, midwives, and composting will become common. There will be two chickens in every garage. What is comes down to is that the Great Leap Backward is very similar to what the environmentalists want, which is really nothing but planned underdevelopment.

To pay for and administer all these public works projects, the Zen socialist government could simply cut the Pentagon down to size. After resigning as a superpower, we certainly won't need a quarter of a trillion dollars a year for our military. We could cut 90 percent of that budget to pay for health care, education, transit, and environmental clean-up.

The other 10 percent of the military's budget should be enough to support a small standing army to help out in hurricanes and other natural disasters, with enough funds left over to keep a few Trident submarines in operation—just in case the Azerbaijanis get some wild ideas about attacking us.

Finally, here is a scheme that will enable the United States to earn foreign revenue as we move from superpower to ordinary nationhood. Consider the fact that we are the most "entertaining" people on the planet, and that the whole world loves American show business. Remember also that many other nations now have more disposable income than we do. So, when we resign as a superpower we simultaneously announce the biggest tourist promotion in history, inviting the rest of the world to come and witness the world's first decline and slide. We turn the country into an entertainment complex, a theme park called Formerly Great America. People would surely pay admission to see this turning point in history. The downhill rides would be spectacular. The possibilities are endless.

At this point we have nothing to lose but our golden chains. Why not go for it? If we put our minds and hearts to it, there is little doubt that we can make the United States an extraordinary ordinary country, one of the finest on earth. Not a lesser underdeveloped nation seeking more wealth and glory, but a people who are glad to be moving a little slower, content just to be. Go ahead and sleep on this idea. A siesta is definitely part of the plan.

Tribe follows tribe and nation follows nation
like the waves of the sea.
It is the order of nations, and regret is useless.
Your time of decay may be distant but it will surely come,
for even the white man, whose God walked and talked
    with him
as friend with friend, cannot be exempt from
    the common destiny.
We may be brothers after all. We will see.

ATTRIBUTED TO CHIEF SEATTLE, 1855

The "Zen" in Zen socialism is there to remind us that no matter how good our government is, it's important to keep a cosmic perspective handy at all times. One that works especially well for me is also my favorite science story of the past couple of decades—the ongoing debate about the fate of the cosmos.

Although scientists are generally agreed that the big bang sent all of the universe's matter and energy expanding outward at great speed, they still don't agree on where it will end up. If the expansion continues, the theory goes, then the universe will just thin out into nothingness, a fate which astrophysicists call "cold death." The only alternative is "heat death," which would occur if there was enough mass in the universe and therefore enough gravity, to slow the expansion down. Then all the matter-energy, and space-time as well, would eventually be pulled back together into one tiny subatomic particle. The scientists call this process of contraction the big crunch, as opposed to the big bang. The big crunch sounds like a good name for a candy bar—perhaps a densely packed nugget of black-hole colored chocolate. So which would you rather have, a crunch—or nothingness? Heat death or cold death? Depending on its design, the universe will get us coming or going. The scientists themselves still go back and forth, so to speak, on what our fate will be.

I'm sure the universe pays very little attention to my desires, but I personally favor the big crunch, because it would mean that we (matter-energy) all might come together again, and then explode in another big bang. When the Dalai Lama was asked whether Tibetan Buddhists have a big bang in their cosmology, he replied, "Oh yes, but it is 'bang, bang, bang.' There are many big bangs. And many universes." Maybe the Tibetans are right, and universes just keep expanding and contracting, over and over again. And maybe the next big bang will explode us into a universe where everything will make more sense, and all the various lifeforms will join together in a harmonious dance of joy. Hope to see you there.

It's fairly obvious that I haven't lost my idealism. My great American dreams somehow turned into a Zen socialist utopia, and even a brand new universe! At least I have pretty much given up hope that I will get enlightened in this lifetime. The attitude of hope, however, is considered one of the last barriers to enlightenment, so maybe giving up hope will take me over the top.

Even if none of my great American dreams come true, I still consider myself fortunate. "We live like kings here," as my father used to say. If the Buddha were alive, he'd probably tell me that I indeed have a lucky birth, and remind me that even here in late twentieth-century America, his teaching is still about the "middle path," the way lies somewhere between all the extremes. He would also, no doubt, encourage me to continue meditating. One of the best ways I can help myself and the planet is to sit and be still for a while everyday. There is too much waving of hands going on, and that only leads to more frustration and global warming.

In the end, while I still consider myself a cynic in recovery, I sincerely give thanks for being born into this transitional era. The cracks in our civilization have at least given me the opportunity to see through them. As usual, our dilemmas are also our deliverance.

Remembering that, have a nice millenium. And if you don't like the news, go out and make some of your own.